Philippa Merivale is a member of the Teaching Faculty of the International Academy of Colour Therapeutics, which is based in Lincolnshire. She has worked as a consultant and teacher in a number of different countries, and her work abroad is focused in the Far East and Eastern Europe.

HEALING WITH COLOUR

An Experience of Aura-Soma

Philippa Merivale

E L E M E N T

Shaftesbury, Dorset • Boston, Massachusetts
Melbourne, Victoria

© Element Books Limited 1998
Text © Philippa Merivale 1998

The author and publishers gratefully acknowledge permission to
include an extract from *An Evil Cradling* by Brian Keenan
(Random House, 1992)

First published in UK in 1998 by
Element Books Limited
Shaftesbury, Dorset SP7 8BP

Published as *Healing with Color* in the USA in 1998 by
Element Books, Inc.
160 North Washington Street,
Boston, Massachusetts 02114

Published in Australia in 1998 by
Element Books and distributed
by Penguin Australia Limited
487 Maroondah Highway, Ringwood,
Victoria 3134

Reprinted 1998

Cover design by Slatter–Anderson
Illustrations by Michela Ducco
Photographs reproduced by permission of Aura–Soma UK
Page design by Mark Slader
Typeset by Bournemouth Colour Press

Printed and bound in Great Britain by
J. W. Arrowsmith Ltd, Bristol
in the USA by Edwards Brothers Inc, Michigan

British Library Cataloguing in Publication
data available

ISBN 1 86204 400 7

For Mike

The day will come when,
after harnessing space,
the winds, the tides and
gravitation, we shall harness
for God the energies of love.
And on that day, for the
second time in the history
of the world, we shall have
discovered fire.

Teilhard de Chardin

CONTENTS

ACKNOWLEDGEMENTS

To all those many people who provided help and support through some very difficult years, in ways too numerous to recount, I offer my deepest thanks. It is not possible to name more than a few of these friends, colleagues, and members of my family individually. Most of them will, I hope, know that they are recognized.

In particular I wish to thank my cousin, Professor Patricia Merivale, and my two long-suffering sisters Ann Merivale and Alexandra Van Duivenbode: also my friends Polly Willmington, Erik Pelham, William Grey-Campbell, Kathleen Colhoun and Lizzie Webster. Claudia Booth is acknowledged within the text, but the depth and constancy of her love and support have gone way beyond anything described therein. Aaron Booth also deserves thanks far deeper than has been indicated in the story. Thank you, Aaron. And thanks to Judy Marshall, whose initiative in an emergency has already been publicly acknowledged by the award of a medal.

For the more specific help which I received in putting together this book, I owe an enormous debt of thanks to The Hon. James Mackay who offered me not only a home for as long as the need might continue, but also swift and acute editorial criticism and unconditional encouragement. Edwyn Courtenay also shared with me some profound insights when I first started to explore the world of colour, a few of which are indirectly quoted within the text. Edwyn also drew the original auric pictures of Magdalen from which the artist has created those which appear in the text. Susan Lascelles, my editor at Element, has offered invaluable guidance and help in focusing my intent.

I offer my thanks, too, to Michela Ducco, whose illustrations have given visual support to the text.

I am also grateful to my students and clients, so many of whom have taught me so much. Every consultation and every workshop, for me as well as, I hope, for them, is a gift and a learning experience.

The greatest thanks of all, for what they have lived through and taught me, go to my three children, Nicola, Stephen and Magdalen; and finally to Mike Booth, my teacher, mentor, doctor and friend, without whom this book would never have been thought of, and to whom it is dedicated.

A NOTE ON CASE HISTORIES

Those referred to in the case histories have all been given English names, though in fact the stories have been gathered from people of different nationalities. In order to preserve their anonymity, the details have been altered. Nevertheless, the core of each story remains, in order to illustrate the essence of the colour which they describe.

FOREWORD

You will gather from the content of this book that I know Philippa very well. I have been fortunate enough to witness her growth in the context of *Aura-Soma* and also what she has been able to present from her own inner being to the world through *Aura-Soma*.

It gives me great pleasure to be able to write a brief Foreword to this book. What is contained here is something which fits into the body of information about *Aura-Soma* very appropriately; and it is my hope that many will be touched by the words which Philippa offers. She has a gift for communication; and that communication is not a dry one from the intellect but something which comes from her heart. Her quality is contained within this book. This may well be the first of her writings as she begins to express the offering that comes through her to the world.

Philippa's insight and experience in teaching *Aura-Soma* in various parts of the world have given her some perspectives which, I believe, will be of benefit not only to the general reader or the beginner in *Aura-Soma*, but also to those who have gone deeper and practised as consultants themselves. The information within the text is at once accessible, and yet has an element of depth which rewards further consideration.

As Principal of the Aura-Soma International Academy of Colour Therapeutics, which is based here in Tetford with branches in Texas, USA, and Coff's Harbour, Australia, I would have no hesitation in recommending this text as being beneficial to *Aura-Soma* practitioners throughout the world.

Philippa has been instrumental in spreading the practice of *Aura-Soma*, particularly in Japan and in what used to be called Russia, where she continues to bring inspiration and understanding of colour as consciousness. This book may be of benefit to anyone interested in colour and *Aura-Soma* as a therapeutic system, or interested in light in relation to the coming times for mankind and the planet. *Aura-Soma* has a role to play in the development of consciousness at this time: through Philippa's words and what it is that she offers here I am sure that many will be inspired to look deeper into this system of colour and light.

Thank you, Philippa, for the opportunity to participate in your process and for the teachings you have offered me.

MIKE BOOTH
Principal
The Aura-Soma International Academy
of Colour Therapeutics

INTRODUCTION

If you pick up and open this book I invite you, dear reader, to join me on a voyage of discovery which began some years ago. It was a voyage which took me through a series of bizarre and gruelling events, before eventually leading to astonishing and colourful pastures. The journey was arduous and intense; it involved deep and excruciating pain; yet ultimately the experience was one of revelation and joy.

This book, which essentially is about colour, is the product of that journey. It tells of a voyage, literally, from a labyrinth of darkness and confusion and despair to a whole new world of colour and light.

For several years since the early events recorded in these pages, I have worked as a teacher and practitioner of colour therapy; but this is not a textbook. In fact, one of the effects of writing it has been to show me how little I, or most of us except for a few exceptional beings endowed with the rarest of gifts, can really know of the infinite details of the mysterious workings of the universe. It is, rather, an attempt to share my experience and thus to offer you a little glimpse of what I can truly say I experienced as enlightenment. Where theory creeps into the text, as it inevitably will every so often, it is because the revelations of colour and light are so exciting! It is hard to resist, from time to time, the temptation to try to share a passion, to explain what we believe we may have learned; just as we long to share a new discovery in music or a good film.

What this text sets out to offer, essentially, is a portrait. It offers a suggestion of why it is that the energies of light and colour have such a remarkable effect on our well-being and on our understanding. It invites you, through words and pictures, to perceive the energies of colour in a new way. This way may inspire you to continue the search for yourself, along whichever path is yours. It may prompt you to re-paint the walls of your living-room, or to embark on a deep search for self-discovery, or simply to buy a different coloured soap or a new silk scarf. It really doesn't matter.

As you read I would ask you to set aside for the moment, as I had to, your rational mind, and any previous knowledge; because it seems to me that the rational mind frequently suffers from a need to impose control on a universe which is not subject to such domination. If we can let go of our need for control, we can open ourselves to receive. For some of us this may be a novel experience! The universe, contrary to what many of us think, is benign and unconditionally generous. Allowing ourselves to receive from this limitless source of light, and of love, is like coming out of a damp cave into the warm sunshine. Maybe at first the light is a little dazzling; but our eyes become accustomed to it soon enough.

We cannot control and dominate the universe. Indeed a great deal of suffering has been caused by our attempts to do so. Nor can most human beings, with the partial limitations of time and space to which we are subject, grasp the finer details of the way in which this great universe lives and works. The simplifications in this text are conscious and deliberate. We can, however, learn to understand something of the universal structure. We can discover that this structure is governed and supported by great spiritual laws. Nothing happens by chance; there is nothing haphazard; no good luck or bad luck. It has been calculated, for example, that if the earth were 1 per cent further away from the sun it would be frozen; if it were 5 per cent nearer it would evaporate. Here is an illustration of the precise way in which our universe has been structured. The laws of the universe are the laws by which we live, whether we realize it or not. Here is the exciting prospect: an understanding of colour can lead us towards a way of working in harmony with these universal or natural laws which govern the universe and our lives. Once we begin to see and understand the workings of these laws and apply them consciously to the way we live, we can co-operate with them rather than wasting energy in attempting to swim against the tide. Then we can find love and harmony and peace and health.

In setting aside some of the demands of the rational mind I would prefer to offer a definition of understanding which has reference to our experience: 'Our feet are our under-standing'. I am not a scientist; and the conviction behind any of the theories propounded in these pages comes not from what I have read or studied but from what I have lived. These are living energies described here, incorporated in the experiences of the living I have done. If colour be the food of love (which, along with music, I believe it is), read on.

Teaching and consulting have taken me to many different parts of the world. Often I work with people of whose language I do not speak or understand a word. It could, on the face of it, be most awfully frustrating. There is not the suggestion of any of the usual cushions of comfort that we easily fall back on in our everyday dealings with people: none of the small-talk we often reach for is a first encounter, nor is there any hope of a normal conversation. Frequently the limit of our shared vocabulary is 'hello'. The only hope I have of communicating with the clients or the students is through the interpreter, and through an array of glass bottles containing the most beautiful colours this side of Paradise. Thus, aside from the translator, we are dependent entirely on the universal language of colour. Everywhere the message that comes back is the same: 'We have,' they tell us, 'tried many different forms of counselling. But nothing goes as deep as this.'

Why might this be? This is what, in these pages, I hope to convey. So many people are searching. They are searching for answers and they hardly know where to begin. Often they have not even discovered what the problem is. Colour can show us new avenues we never dared to hope for. The reason is that colour speaks to us at the deepest level of our consciousness. It is a language way beyond words. Nevertheless, words can help us to find the way towards its meaning. An understanding of the language of colour can help us to find the answers which have lain hidden within the depths of our soul. We are each responsible for ourselves and our own destiny. Many factors influence us: our relationships, our environment, even the phases of the moon. Yet nothing in the end has a greater significance in the path of our life than our own will, and the power of our thought.

This may be expressed in another way: by whatever it is that we think, we create our own reality! The quality of the energy which we radiate comes back to us as experience. This is a natural law. Working with colour can help us to become aware of that quality, the energy which we radiate, and to modify it. In other words it can help us to recognize and accept ourselves with all our unconscious tendencies and patterns of behaviour. The strange thing is that it is only when we accept ourselves as we are that we are free to change. We can let go of old patterns. We can kick the fear and do it anyway, whatever it is. We can take back our power. If we create our own reality we may as well make it a good one! So, little by little, we may learn to take responsibility for our destiny, open ourselves to receive, and accept a life of beauty and abundance.

Colour opens doors to hidden rooms within ourselves. It shows us a gentle route towards our own unconscious, wherein lie so many of the answers to life's difficulties: thus it carries the keys to our empowerment. *Aura-Soma*, the system of colour therapy described in these pages, is a means through which we may modify our consciousness, raise our perceptions, and thus enrich our lives.

THE WINDS OF CHANGE

There is a legend told of St Francis of Assisi. It was midwinter, cold and frosty, and not a leaf in sight. He called out to an almond tree: 'Talk to me of God!' The almond tree responded by bursting into bloom. From every branch there leapt forth leaves and blossom.

This rather startling story gives us a vivid illustration of the constant outpouring of the energy which comes from somewhere, perpetually creating and recreating the physical world. As long as there is life there is movement of energy. Here, as so often, that energy is expressed as colour. The spring and summer are the time of year when the creative force is at its most active, and colour abounds throughout the natural world. We refer to the 'full blossoming' of youth and the 'full flowering' of adulthood: those times when we are at our most powerful and creative.

Most of us are aware of our favourite colours. Do you find that those colours vary at different phases of your life, or with differing moods? Many people, if they start to think about it, observe that their thoughts and feelings and even some of their experiences are marked by colour. A 'grey day' does not mean only that it is raining. Do you associate different colours with the seven days of the week? For many children, for example, Saturdays represent relaxation and fun and take on a bright cheerful colour, whereas their least favourite day is associated with dull grey or black. Colour is used consciously by those in power, be they advertisers or politicians, and unconsciously by all of us in our language. We refer to 'feeling in the pink' when all is going well, or to 'having the blues' when we feel depressed. We refer to a healthy burst of anger as 'seeing red', or to a more destructive, less easily expressed, perhaps continued state of anger as a 'black rage'. We describe people as being 'green' with envy or jealousy, or 'yellow bellied' when we mean that they lack courage. The essence of all these phrases, with very few exceptions, is much the same whether we are communicating in English, German, Japanese, or any other language. The reason is that they describe changes which take place in the aura, or the light around the body, with changes in our state of mind or heart or body.

Children have a naturally acute awareness of colour. How many fond parents have spent a small fortune on a beautiful new outfit from their favourite children's clothing shop, only to have it cast aside in favour of the neighbour's gaudy cast-off T-shirt?

Patients suffering from severe depressive illness describe their world as being completely grey: all colour disappears. Accident victims, on the other hand, and others recovering from close encounters with death, when their perceptions are heightened, are acutely colour conscious. When people are fortunate enough to dream in colour they are aware that those dreams are especially vivid.

The post-war England of the 1950s lacked colour. Crockery and furnishings and clothing were functional rather than visual. As energy has returned into individuals and the economy, the material world has grown more and more colourful. Television and cinema have moved into glorious technicolour, and this colour is moving into the world of computers and even, in some cases, into communication by telephone. We are able, if we choose, to wear and to surround ourselves with more vivid and vibrant colours perhaps than at any other time in history. Advances in technology are invariably accompanied by advances in the use of colour. This is paralleled, it seems, by the fact that increases in consciousness are marked by increases in awareness of colour. The most primitive societies saw only in black and white. As consciousness developed more colours became available to the human eye.

In his book *An Evil Cradling*, Brian Keenan talks about his experience as a hostage. A day came when the prison wardens left a bowl of fruit in his cell:

> But wait. My eyes are almost burned by what I see. There's a bowl in front of me that wasn't there before. A brown button bowl and in it some apricots, some small oranges, some nuts, cherries, a banana. The fruits, the colours, mesmerise me in a quiet rapture that spins through my head. I am entranced by colour. I lift an orange into the flat filthy palm of my hand and feel and smell and lick it. The colour orange, the colour, the colour, my God the colour orange. Before me is a feast of colour. I feel myself begin to dance, slowly, I am intoxicated by colour. I feel the colour in a quiet somnambulant rage. Such wonder, such absolute wonder in such an insignificant fruit.

A few years ago I ran into a therapy which over the last 14 years has grown from the quiet activities of a semi-retired blind healer to a fully-fledged therapeutic system currently practised in over 40 countries. It has helped millions of people all over the world. Within the years since I came across this system, which is called *Aura-Soma*, it has turned my life around. As the

3

core of this therapy is contained within a range of little glass bottles of two-coloured liquids, the possibility that this could do much for individuals or the world would have seemed to me, at first, more than a little unlikely. So I would like to recount something of the circumstances and events which brought me to discover a profound healing tool, which indeed goes far beyond the confines of what we would normally term a healing tool, or system, as I believe that these colours, and the language of colour, contain a gift which is there for anyone who cares to take a closer look.

THE JOURNEY BEGINS

In the summer of 1990 my husband and I moved, with our three young children, from the centre of the bustling university town, Oxford, to the depths of rural Lincolnshire, the remote English county devoted almost entirely to the cultivation of crops. There followed a period of change and trauma way beyond my wildest forebodings. I had loved Oxford, and to contemplate leaving it was painful. On the other hand for so long everything had been going wrong: I got parking tickets and punctures; my car broke down, usually at night in winter; if we went on holiday you could be sure at least one person would go down with gastric flu; there was never enough money. As for my husband, well he was rarely at home, at least not when it mattered. When the ceiling had fallen down he was thousands of miles away; by the time he came home the builders and I had finished the reparation and everything was beautiful. I was always alone, except for my friends. I was searching, I knew not for what: rather vaguely I had always hoped that a happy husband and an end to money worries would solve all ills.

We had been offered the prospect of shifting everything to Lincolnshire, a north-eastern county far from anywhere, with no university and no motorway, few cars and fewer people. I was in pursuit of family happiness. I reasoned that, while the children and I would miss our many good friends, we should be compensated by relative financial ease, and by 'quality time' as a family. Besides, I had played the role of the good wife for so long I had forgotten any other. Privately I dreaded the isolation. I had never been one for village life. My preconception of social life in rural communities was of bring-and-buy sales in the local church hall: home-made jams, bottled plums and seedlings. I happened to be interested in none of these things. The countryside, in my reckoning, was fine for nurturing flax and wheat, but not for people. Even so, somehow or other, I thought, I would cope.

In fact, the move was my last-ditch attempt to save my marriage. Always given to extreme solutions, I knew that this move offered my husband the chance at last to live out his long-standing fantasy about country living. Here was the possibility of a house with eighteen acres between us and the nearest neighbour. That, however, would come later, after the auction. Meanwhile, we moved into a housing estate on the outer edges of a small market town, anonymous and vaguely porridge-coloured. It was bordered on one side by fields which stretched endlessly into the distance, and on the other by rows of similar houses which sprawled their way towards the periphery of what was to be our new home town. This little town had 40 or 50 shops, perhaps a thousand or two people, and a few pubs, in one of which the local Dramatic Society staged their annual play. Any traffic jams were caused by slow-moving tractors and the chief road hazard, it seemed then, was caused by the mud off the back of their trailers.

For several months our little rented pocket-size house was home. The porridge colour of the estate reminded me dimly of Purgatory. Heaven, in my mind, had – as far back into childhood as I could remember – always been a comfortable establishment, with colours which were warm, if a little lavish

5

for the middle classes; and Hell, by contrast, had been thoroughly black. Purgatory, colour-wise, had been neither here nor there: it was a place where you waited for something to happen. Boring but safe. It only occurred to me much later that Purgatory means purgative: purging and cleansing; clearing out the old way of being to make way for something else.

Then the dream house came up for auction. It was a Georgian farmhouse surrounded by eighteen acres of rough grass and woodland. Or rather it had been. Its previous owners had for some mysterious reason decided that it was wasteful to have too many rooms and so removed the back half of the house, leaving the inner walls to serve as protection against the ferocious climate. It was like a down-market version of Wuthering Heights: windswept and bleak. But it was but ripe for conversion: it had that quality, so prized by estate agents the world over, 'potential'. We bought it not for what it was but for what it might become. From the full security of our little porridge-coloured house I planned the colours of carpets and curtains, walls and doors. With a beautiful townhouse such as ours to sell, I felt confident of the security and comfort of our economic future, if not our personal one.

I went out and bought two ponies. For someone who was not into country living this was perhaps going a bit over the top; but horses had been the frustrated passion of my childhood (even my name means lover of horses, and loved *by* horses). Our nearly teenage daughter was horse mad. I felt guilty at dragging her away from a life she loved; perhaps some unconscious part of my mind already knew that what we were transporting her towards would be something of a nightmare rather than a pleasant summer's dream. Besides, if we were going to do this country living thing we were going to do it properly.

Unfortunately, we lacked the wisdom to sell one house

before buying another. Our Oxford house had seemed to be such a safe bet. We planned to sell it for a sum with which we could not only buy the farmhouse outright, but convert it to comfortable modernity. The house in Oxford was in a perfect spot with easy access to everything that anyone would want. That was what the squatters thought too. They moved in as frequently as we moved them out, causing devastation and chaos on each of their visits. We discovered that there was a squatters' estate agency. If your house once got on to their books they acted like greased lightning: every time a tenant moved out to make way for a prospective buyer the back door was smashed and the next company of squatters moved in. Then the property market collapsed. Paying for houses both in Oxford and Lincolnshire, we were soon well established on the road to financial ruin. The marriage, rickety at the best of times, staggered and collapsed under the strain.

Prior to this, in the middle of December we had moved in to the farmhouse, horses and all. It turned out to be the severest winter the area had know for many years. We had had the house gutted before moving in, and the plan was for the building work to continue through the winter. That, however, was not to be. Six months had soon elapsed after the initial move to the housing estate and the Oxford house was still unsold. Long before the end of the winter the money ran out and the builders went home, leaving us with a gap of several inches between the tops of the bare walls and the roof. My husband, who never felt the cold, went off and spent each day in a centrally heated office. I rather wondered what to do with myself. I did not know anyone. The well, which was our only source of water, had run dry. The snow drove relentlessly on and the only form of heating was open grates in the downstairs rooms. I had never been especially keen on camping, even in the sunshine. When the temperature inside the kitchen registered −13°C (the temperature outside being merely

−12°C) the going was getting tough; but we were in it by then and there was no clear escape route. I returned one day from driving the children to school and stood in the kitchen, scarved and cloaked, wondering about a strategy for surviving the next few hours. Fetching sticks to light a fire meant going out in the snow again, with the full force of the wind, and I was too cold for that. There was nowhere to go so I stood for a while, hoping to muster up the courage to build a fire. Then I passed out. When I came to again it was past lunch time. Half a day nearer to springtime.

This was only the beginning. The real tests still lay ahead; but it was at this time that I first met Mike and Claudia Booth. As the sun receded further and further into the winter sky and the temperature dropped daily a little lower, so our domestic economy and morale were grinding to a halt. The isolation was as relentless as the winter. It was a relief to get to know Claudia, whom in some way I felt I recognized, though we had never met properly. When we did come to meet we discovered that we had lived a few hundred yards from each other in Oxford ten years before, when our eldest children had been toddlers.

THE DISCOVERY OF *AURA-SOMA*

The first time I visited Claudia she told me that her husband, who was 'a kind of healer, I suppose', was very preoccupied with Vicky Wall, an elderly lady with whom they had been closely involved over the previous five years, who was dying. She also recounted something of another event in their lives: two years previously, her husband's son by his former marriage, Aaron, had been hit by a lorry. Aaron had only recently emerged from a coma and was severely damaged physically and living in a wheelchair. They were therefore very much taken up with Aaron's needs, as well as those of the elderly friend, Vicky.

Nevertheless, a few days later Claudia introduced me to her husband, Mike. We spoke perhaps a dozen words each. This is a trifling event; yet I remember every detail of my early connection with both Claudia and with Mike. At some level I knew immediately that this connection marked the beginning of a new phase in my life. When they invited us for a meal it felt like a warm hearth in midwinter in more ways than one.

Mike and Claudia took us that day to visit Dev Aura, which had been the Rectory in Tetford, the village where we all lived. Vicky Wall had just died. Vicky had bought the Rectory a few years previously in a state of dereliction and a small group consisting of Vicky's friends had restored it to its present state with the intention of making it into some kind of teaching centre. In fact the teaching had already begun. We watched a video film of Vicky Wall conversing with a group of students, gathered from several different parts of the globe. She was talking to them about colour. We looked around the house, and the beautiful garden, and at a display of glass bottles containing highly coloured liquids. These liquids were in two fractions: an oily fraction resting on one of herbal waters, so that the majority of the bottles were of two contrasting colours. There were around eighty of them and they had a name: '*Balance*'.

I have often heard, in the course of meeting people from all corners of the world since that time, of their response when meeting the *Aura-Soma Balance* bottles for the first time. Many people are lyrical about it. They talk about rainbows. They talk about coming home. Many of them seem to have known from that first moment that these bottles are calling them and they go to enormous lengths to find ways of attending the courses and pursuing what grows very rapidly into a passion. For me, I must confess, there was none of this. Maybe my mind and my emotions were locked up by years of suppression; maybe they were frozen by the cold. I found the colours extremely beautiful, but in at once stepped my rational sceptical mind to put a stop to any intuitive response. I can still see clearly in my mind the room in which we were shown the *Balance* bottles, and even the wall against which the shelves stood. Some elusive part of my consciousness was touched, and moved; but the movement was so slight as to be imperceptible. Like the minute hand of a watch, only in retrospect can we see that it has moved at all. My rational mind was in charge here: it came in with a polite dismissive laugh. The colours were, of course, wonderful; but the idea of basing any kind of healing system on pretty potions and lotions was simplistic.

I had a short conversation with Mike that evening in which I asked him something about his work; how he spent his time; how he made a living. I knew already that he was some kind of a healer but I could not see where these little bottles fitted in. 'Were the bottles his main occupation?' I asked him, privately wondering what on earth he did with them.

'Well we've got a choice haven't we?' Mike replied quietly. 'We are at a crossroads; we can go one of two ways. Either we go on the way we have done and destroy ourselves. Or we can go in a new direction.'

This was not the answer I expected. I glimpsed at only a fraction of his meaning; and I could not relate that meaning to the bottles. As Mike wrote to me years later: 'We cannot push the river. It flows at its own pace.'

Mike talked a very little about the *Balance* bottles, in answer to my questions. He told me that for the first time in a system of healing these bottles brought back together all the characteristics of the plant in one single package: the water ingredient, the oil ingredient, and the colour. The water ingredient contained the herbal essences, as used in herbal medicine; the oil ingredient contained the essential oils which are used in aromatherapy. All of this came together in a healing system whose language is colour.

For the moment that was it. I was preoccupied with the arduous business of survival, carrying water from a tap the other end of a field, building fires to ward off the paralyzing cold. For a few months I put the visit to Dev Aura into a drawer inside my mind and got on with the gardening: planting shrubs which would do their best in these merciless winds, which would perhaps dig deep in to the soil in an attempt to find sustenance. They would, like us, build for the future. What about the present? The winds swept on, rushing down the hill towards us and swirling around the house with all the force of a full gale. These were the winds of change all right. Was this really my attempt to save the marriage? It was rather, perhaps, a death wish, someone suggested: the welcoming of discomfort so extreme that our domestic arrangements must surely break and change. What else would induce anyone to embrace such hostile ground?

These months were made much more sustainable than they might have been by the fact that Mike Booth had for some reason taken it upon himself to offer me regular treatment. It was an extraordinary gift. He offered me not just homoeopathy or adjustments to my spine – and with my high stress levels I was profoundly grateful for this alone. But what he gave me in addition to all this was something new, and completely unexpected: it was healing on a level I had never guessed at. Mike offered me a quality of unconditional love within which I felt absolutely safe: an unconditional acceptance which allowed things to be, exactly as they were. Yet within this space he challenged me on the deepest level, urging me to take responsibility for every last detail in my life. 'When the student is ready,' he told me, 'the teacher appears.'

It was a long long winter. Compassionate relatives had us connected to the mains water supply, and we equipped ourselves with an ancient but still functional Rayburn heater. As long as we remembered to keep fuelling it it deposited a fine layer of coal dust all over the house and provided lashings of hot water. This was luxury; and it was just as well as late winter brought us to the state described by the lawyers as 'irretrievable breakdown of marriage'. I woke up in the middle of one memorable night and found myself next to the person I had married and could no longer take it even when the poor man was asleep. As it was two o'clock in the morning there was nowhere to go, so I crawled off to the bath, much comforted by the frequent replenishments of hot water. That was where I spent the rest of the night.

If much of my inspiration and strength came as a gift from Mike, my comfort for the main part came from the children. While my eldest, Nicola, had found Lincolnshire life and all that went with it intolerable, and been rescued by a fairy godmother who returned her to her much-loved Oxford school as a boarder, my son, Stephen, had rapidly overcome his initial rejection of the culture shock and acquired a steady group of footballing friends. My littlest, Magdalen, was by now five: she had never really had any problem with any of it. She had marked her arrival in the nursery school two years earlier by her solo performance of 'Twinkle Twinkle Little Star' in the Christmas concert, and had never looked back. Knowing that somehow or other through all this they all three grew steadily stronger, I was able, little by little, to let go of some of the anxiety and parental guilt I had felt about the difficulties to which they had been subjected, and to begin to turn some of my attention to other things. Exhausted, and bewildered by the apparently endless battering by forces which I did not understand, I was surprised and relieved to discover that English country life sometimes offered more than healthy walks and free-range eggs. Without the support of the international community which was by now thriving around Dev Aura, I would not care to imagine how things might have been. The sessions with Mike continued, regular and reliable.

At his invitation, and with the practical support of Claudia, I attended courses at Dev Aura. I was not clear why it was that Mike was offering me so much education and support, but at the time mine was not to question why. Battered and confused, I accepted with few queries and with considerable relief. For years I had had a vague sense of vocation within the healing sphere. I was accustomed to working with my hands, but only when the occasion required it, having discovered that to do so often relieved people's aches and pains. It was like an automatic switch that was turned on when someone was hurting, but I understood little about regulating it. I had learned some homoeopathy and done a course in therapeutic massage, which I had offered to a few people in my spare time, but that was about as far as it had ever gone.

The effect of the courses at Dev Aura was extraordinary. In this little village, the unlikeliest place in England, were gathered people from all over the world. Like me, they were experiencing something new and very profound. Some of them, like myself, were going through severe difficulties; some were already established therapists from various disciplines; others were designers or artists who wished to find another perspective on colour. They came to Dev Aura from all corners of the globe and for many different reasons. Some came consciously for their own healing and growth, looking for a tool to aid them in their process of evolution; some simply from a vague sense that life held more possibilities than they had been able to access.

What we were learning was a whole new language: the language of colour. It is a universal language, ignoring all barriers of race or culture or creed. It cuts through personality and addresses us at the level of pure consciousness. In recognizing our colour preferences, we began to discover in those workshops something about who we were at the very deepest level. 'You are the colours you choose, and the colours

13

you choose reflect your being's needs.' This is a phrase which is often repeated in *Aura-Soma*, because we are, literally, the colours we choose, and through those colours our unconscious mind can recognize more than any professional therapist can tell us. What we can recognize, with an astonishing degree of accuracy and depth, is ourselves. In this context I began, very dimly at first, to understand the truth of what Mike had for some time been teaching me: that through our unconscious choices we create our own reality, our own experience. Nothing happens by chance. This was a tough idea to chew on, in view of what was still happening around us. Back at the farm things were growing steadily more uncomfortable. It was, as I remember it, winter. Like the garden of Oscar Wilde's selfish giant, it was always winter there.

One of the attractive aspects of the relocation deal which had been offered by my husband's company was a generous allowance for interior furnishings. In my customary enthusiasm I had plunged straight in and ordered new curtains for every room. For the first time in my life I had not even had to make them myself: I had commissioned an interior designer to make the whole lot. So there they hung, ludicrous in all their glory: beautiful fabrics against the grimy background of crumbling plaster and bare bricks. They had not even a full roof to protect them. They represented the remnants of the rosy tint which had for so long coloured our view of our lives. They kept out some of the light but none of the wind. It was, the universe was telling us, time to get real. The most glorious materials in the world could have done nothing to brighten the dismal domestic scene, or the decayed façade of our marriage. Sixteen years of loneliness and abuse, denied and suppressed, while every fibre of my being had cried out for companionship, and a little warmth. Without a structure to support it, the habit of denial was no longer an option.

With the Oxford house well known to all prospective

buyers as a liability, we were losing, every month, an outrageous sum of money. Then one day, out of the blue, I received a cheque. A premium bond which I had been given at birth produced the grand sum of fifty pounds. In terms of our monthly losses, it was a little like being presented with a copper coin. Life had begun to resemble some grotesque game of Monopoly. What was this, I wondered, some cosmic joke? What card were they going to deal next? 'Go to Jail. Do not pass Go. Do not collect £200?' I was not amused.

This was not to say that I had any clearly formulated idea as to who 'they' might be. Cards, it seemed to me, got dealt out at random. I was certain of only one thing: that I was a victim. There was no way that I could be held responsible for any of the surrounding chaos.

It was time for another session with Mike. Thank God, I thought. I suppose I had some vague notion that once I had dumped all this on him he would wave a crystal wand and create a brave new world. I informed him, as the tears rolled down my face, that I was at the end of my tether. 'I see no indication,' Mike replied quietly, 'that you are anywhere near the end of your tether.'

He had come up trumps again. He had offered me precisely the opposite of what I expected to hear. What a blessing that it is not given to us to know what lies ahead. I was indeed only at the very beginning of my tether, did I but know it. Events would prove Mike more accurate than either of us would have liked to imagine.

A few days later Mike invited me on another *Aura-Soma* course.

REBIRTH

The experience of colour and light can work in many different ways. *Balance* itself, that force pack of plant and mineral colour power, can work so quietly behind the scenes that for a while the change is barely perceptible; or it can enter the very cells of consciousness with the speed and the force of lightning. It depends on many things. Perhaps it depends partly on our willingness to change.

The bottles sat serene and quiet on their glass shelves, the focal point of this and every other *Aura-Soma* training course, their colours radiant and joyful, resembling the exotic tones of silks and orchids, precious stones and tropical fish. They glowed and sparkled, iridescent in the light of that room, radiating their warmth and luminescence with the gentle self-assurance of those who know their strength. It was as though each pair of colours, each conjunction of oil and water, had a personality quite different from all the others. As in all strong relationships, each duo of colours shared profound and special secrets. Yet their focus was outwards; they would willingly share their wisdom with those who came towards them with ready ears and an open heart. Colour was the signature of these bottles, and it was their language. They would speak this language, still unfamiliar to many of us, yet one which would cross all barriers of culture or creed, and which was as old as time itself.

Our first task, this and every day, was to choose a small selection of our favourite *Balance* bottles. We had first to choose the single bottle which we liked the most and felt we could happily keep forever; then, the next most favourite, and so on until we had chosen four bottles. The order in which the colours were chosen was as vital as the colours themselves; there was significance, too, in the position of the colours in the top half of any of the bottles in relation to those contained within the base fraction.

The workshop was well under way. This particular one was a gathering of people who were by this time pretty thoroughly versed in this language of colour, and with many and varied skills of their own to bring with them. At this stage I was probably the least experienced in the group. Overwhelmed and exhausted by domestic circumstances, I had given much less than my full attention to the few previous courses which I had attended, returning home at the end of each week's study with a jumble in my head and a set of notes as chaotic as the rest of my life. The situation at home was worse rather than better, but I had started to take notice. One day I asked for special attention. Bewildered and yet fascinated by my selection of some colour combinations which had previously repelled me, I became curious to know what these could possibly mean. Each afternoon there was a 'for instance' group consultation, where all the participants pooled their ideas in response to a particular run of bottles. I asked whether I might offer my selection as a choice for the group that day.

The selection which a client or student makes consists of the four bottles which attracts them most, in order of preference. The first of these is known as the 'Soul bottle', or the 'True Aura bottle', and it gives an indication of the essence of the person choosing it, the life path they have chosen, and their potential. The second then points up the main areas which have caused difficulty in the past, and the gifts to be found when these challenges have been met. The third shows how the person is doing with all this in the present: have some of the main difficulties been dealt with, or are we still stuck with the same issues as before? The fourth then suggests the direction in which we are moving, since by all that we are and do in the present we create, step by step, our future experience.

The bottles are held only by the cap, in order to reduce the interference of our energies with those in the bottle which are delicately balanced. They are also chosen with the left hand. This is important. The left side of the body corresponds with the right side of the brain, which is the receptive intuitive side, whereas the right side of the body/left side of the brain tends to be more controlling.

I brought out the bottles I had chosen and placed them on a table near to where Mike stood, where all the 30-odd students could clearly see them. I returned to my place in the circle and waited for what would come.

What I experienced that afternoon was something which before that day would have been difficult to imagine, but which as a teacher and consultant I have witnessed time and again ever since. With the light and warmth of the midday sun the colours dissolved the crumbling remains of my defences; like Cupid's arrows they pierced the very heart of darkness and fear which lay trapped deep within my being. The pain of a lifetime welled up and spilled out: tears of anger and frustration, bewilderment and confusion erupted in a volcano of grief. It seemed to me that each person in that room held a laser torch which penetrated every corner and every cobweb which had lain hidden in the darkest corners of the depths of my unconscious mind. Yet whatever had been concealed within these corners was dazed only momentarily by the light;

it was scorched only long enough to cry out, to show its recognition of itself. All that had lain comatose underneath the dust blinked and stretched, preparing itself to come out and find the day. The skill and the love of Mike and of all those people in the room whom he had taught were indeed a gift from the Creator; yet they were a gift which is universal. In the end they were simply guiding me towards a looking glass, reflecting back to me all that was revealed by the colours which I had reached for and held.

'All' that had lain comatose revealed? Well, not all: there is always more to do. This is what life is: the living and the processing of experience, revealing richer and richer treasures as, little by little, our perceptions are awakened. One step at a time.

According to natural law – that collection of timeless and fundamental principles upon which the universe is built – we create, by the power of our thoughts and expectations, our own reality; in other words the quality of the energy which we radiate comes boomeranging back to us as the quality of experience which we receive. This has been called the first law of the universe, yet it is often the hardest to grasp, because it is not the *conscious* mind which creates this experience. Very few people, with their conscious minds, will choose, for example, poverty – unless they consciously choose the vocation of a nun or a priest or a monk. Yet, if our unconscious expectation is of poverty and anxiety; if our deep self believes that we are unworthy to receive – then wow, we had better watch out. The human mind is, on average, around 95 per cent *unconscious*. The beauty of working with colour is that it enables us to bring up from that deep unconscious place exactly those issues which are most pertinent to our present situation so that they may be examined and understood. Once we can begin to recognize our own unconscious patterns of thought, we can also begin to take responsibility for the reality which those thoughts create; and little by little we can begin to alter the patterns of thought which have been unhelpful to our growth.

Everything hinged, for that short time, on one particular combination: the bottle which was needed the most contained a deep Violet oil supported from beneath by a well of Gold. Mike suggested that my friend and fellow student, Kathleen, should complete this process there and then by offering me a massage, whereupon I was invited to the treatment room. A process for which we would normally recommend a month was the work of a few minutes, as Kathleen swiftly and lovingly smothered my body with this astonishing emulsion: herbs, oils, crystal wavelengths, aromas and colour fused in a torrent of healing energy. The contents of an entire bottle was soaked up by my skin into the core of my being.

After this very extraordinary hour or so of my life, my appetite, long since lost, returned within minutes. I was ravenously hungry. I consumed a hearty meal and returned to the class. The impact of these relatively few moments is almost impossible to convey. Everything that surrounded me had the freshness of a landscape after a storm: all was glowing and new. In short this marked the beginning of a process in which I never looked back; at least not often, and never for very long. Some door inside the core of my unconscious had been opened, and through it I began to glimpse at a new reality. I had begun to understand that somewhere hidden behind the many pains of our lives there is a plan: that nothing happens by chance. I saw that, as often as not, we enter relationships and other experiences in the dark, following some dimly-lit instinct and slowly groping our way towards understanding. Thinking that we want freedom, we nevertheless create prisons for ourselves until we have learned the lessons of the path we have chosen. My life, like so many, was in crisis; yet the Eastern races have a word for crisis which shows it to us in another way. The word contains two characters: one of them means 'danger'; the other 'hidden opportunity'. In short, every experience is a gift if rightly viewed. 'Pain,' wrote Kahlil Gibran, 'is the breaking of the shell which encloses our understanding.'

The colours I had chosen had revealed to those sensitive to their message a picture, a portrait of my soul and of my being's needs. Softened by the warmth of the energies in the room that day I had no doubt been wide open to receive the fullest impact of the colours once they reached my body. Conditions were ripe for the simultaneous balancing of all the levels: thoughts, feelings, and even my body went into deep metamorphosis, from where they all emerged transformed. Life is a process; a journey. This account is in no way intended to suggest that within the space of an hour or so the necessary work of a lifetime can be completed ... Nevertheless, there are moments when the shift is profound, and permanent. This was one of those.

On the face of it this may look like an extreme case. Looked at within the wider context of humanity at large, it was of course a very mild one. Many workshops, too, support cases much more extreme. But the essence of what is described is universal. All over the world people come, if they are open to it, often for their first encounter with themselves. Or perhaps, more nebulously, it is their first encounter with a quality of love so unconditional, so completely accepting of whatever is, that their selves are, for the first time, able to come out and be seen. All rational or scientific explanations aside, the colours, potentized by the wavelengths and gems of the created natural world, are the direct expression of love. In the atmosphere so created, we are able to receive the messages they offer. These are, after all, the messages which we have chosen for ourselves.

Herein lies a vital key: *Aura-Soma* is the only therapy currently available in which the client provides his own analysis, through the colours chosen, of the situation which he has brought to the consulting room, and in which he also chooses his own remedy. *Aura-Soma* is a self-selective, non-intrusive soul therapy. Nothing is imposed from the outside. The counsellor is there to help the client, but not to choose the client's colours. The client, or the student, invariably chooses the colours relating to those issues which he or she is ready to address at that particular time; and the counsellor merely guides that person towards an understanding of what their own choice of colour reveals. Thus the words the colours inspire often create a profound healing response, setting the scene for the deeper rebalancing which may follow. Words themselves are energy at another level, and they have the power to create a profound response. It is interesting that St John's Gospel opens with the sentence: 'In the beginning was the Word'. The Word, in this context, is the thought of God, or of the loving mind behind the universe, made manifest.

The application of *Balance* thus works in harmony with the words of the counsellor to set in motion a powerful and subtle process of restoring equilibrium.

So what exactly are these *Balance* bottles? Rectangular glass bottles containing beautiful colours. This is clearly not the end of the story. People had come to this corner of one of the most remote counties in England because by one means or another they had discovered that these little bottles contained something unique. What was this something? And how could that something have such an astonishing effect on rebalancing the energy, the emotions, and indeed the very spirit of those coming to seek its aid?

There are many answers to this question. Most of them are way beyond the scope of this book. Perhaps part of the answer, however, lies in the mystery through which *Aura-Soma* came to be 'birthed' at all.

COLOUR MEDICINE

*B*alance was born in inspiration, through meditation. Vicky Wall, the blind healer endowed with such exceptional gifts (her physical blindness had been followed by a ten-fold increase in her auric sight), had been in her customary meditative state one night in the last phase of her life when she was asked to 'go divide the waters'. At the same time as receiving this message, she saw waves of colour coming towards her. Diabetic, blind, retired (as she had thought), and with only a small part of her heart function remaining after a heart attack, she did not welcome this request. Replying rather indignantly that she was not Moses, she asked the voices please to leave her alone. Instead, however, they persisted through three nights, at the end of which Vicky found that she had created the first few of these combinations of plant oil balanced over herbal waters, in astonishing colours.

This was a singular way to start a healing system. Vicky, at this stage, had no idea that this – a healing tool – was what these would become. She looked at what had come through her hands as she worked, and she had no idea what purpose these bottles might serve. She discussed this new arrival with her friend and colleague Margaret Cockbain, and they surmised that perhaps they were some kind of beauty oil. A little later, when Vicky had continued the process so that the range of colours had started to expand, they decided to exhibit the bottles at the Subud World Congress, as Vicky had recently become friendly with members of this organization. This was essentially a collection of spiritually minded people who embraced equally all world religions, and it is significant that it was at this event that *Balance* was first displayed to the public, since this underpins the universal nature of the philosophy which has since grown and developed within and around *Aura-Soma*.

WHAT IS *AURA-SOMA*?

Within this question, asked by so many puzzled but interested newcomers, there often lies another question: 'Is it some kind of religion?'

The answer to this question seems vital because of the point in history we have reached. No, *Aura-Soma* is not a religion. Yet it was received in meditation by a woman from a strictly orthodox Jewish family, of which the father had been a master of Kabbalism, that ancient Jewish sub-sect, the knowledge and many thousands of years of study of which had always been available only to men. For Vicky Wall to be excluded in her childhood and teens from this study, which her beloved father had been allowed to share only with his sons, had been a source of considerable grief. Her faith, and her love of her 'Father', by which she might equally mean within one breath either her earthly father or the Creator, was the centre and the focus of her life. Herself pursuing the unusual path of converting from Judaism to Christianity, and then reverting at the end of her life to Judaism, proves how in one way her own denomination is unimportant. The Psalms were her constant companion and she knew every chapter of the Bible; but she was also well versed in The Koran and the essence of most of the other major world religions. The birth of *Balance* came soon after her father's death, and she believed that part of what was happening was that her father was communicating to her something of that knowledge and understanding which he had been unable to do during his lifetime: a wisdom which has its source way back in the annals of time.

So *Aura-Soma* was born in mystery, and the energies which are harnessed within it are ones which have not been understood in the West for several thousands of years. *Aura-Soma* itself, however, is not a religion. It is, in a nutshell, a means by which we may come to a deeper understanding of ourselves than we have previously found, through the recognition of colour. It is thus much simpler than a religion: it has no rules, no dogma, no membership. Yet because it embraces and draws upon the knowledge and understanding contained within many ancient systems of wisdom, while espousing none of them, it gives us access to sources of understanding which are manifold and far-reaching. While *Aura-Soma* has grown and developed to discover many of these sources, there is surely much more still to be revealed.

Colour relates directly to the very essence of our nature. What Vicky Wall had birthed that night was the first part of a tool which has been given to the world at a time of enormous change as we leave behind the Age of Pisces and enter the Age of Aquarius. This new time, I would suggest, presents us with several major challenges, of which two are particularly pertinent in this connection: we need to learn, each one of us, to take responsibility for ourselves rather than refer to an outside source of authority; and, if we wish for the survival of ourselves and our planet, we need to communicate with each other from a point of truth through an open heart. These things are only possible if we know who we are. How can we accept responsibility for ourselves if we do not know what it is for which we are responsible? And how can we communicate openly and truthfully if we do not know who we are?

Aura-Soma, then, I would suggest at this point, is a means whereby we may first recognize our true colours and thus become more deeply acquainted with ourselves. Then, as practitioners, it equips us with the means to offer a great gift to those with whom we come into contact: the possibility of giving people back to themselves. Furthermore, its inception came through a woman towards the end of a time which had for several thousand years been predominantly patriarchal, and it offers to all of us, men and women, the opportunity to awaken to the aspect of ourselves which so often has lain dormant: the feminine, intuitive, receptive, creative aspect.

One particular friend whom Vicky Wall found within the Subud organization was Laura Fraser, who later received, also in meditation, the name for what was beginning to emerge as a system of healing: '*Aura-Soma*'. Nothing happens by chance: the name is significant, acknowledging as it does the workings of energies which have only recently been rediscovered after many years in which they were shrouded in mystery. For colour healing is among the most ancient practices in the world. Archaeological discoveries have shown that some of the healing temples of ancient Egypt were constructed in such a way as to divide the spectrum of white light, so that each room within the temple received a different ray or colour. A healer-priest would bathe his patient in the colour of which he perceived that person to have the greatest need. Other methods involved soaking in coloured waters.

Aura in Latin means the light, the personal colour which signifies our soul purpose. It also means breeze; a slight movement of air. *Soma* derives from several sources: from Greek it means body; from Aramaic it means the being; and from Sanskrit it means living energies. So *Aura-Soma* means the light, the colour, the living, moving energies of the being incarnate.

Both Vicky Wall and Mike Booth, who at Vicky's request came with Claudia to join her in her work a couple of years after the birth of *Balance*, had been gifted since early childhood with auric sight, which enabled them to see the colours of the energy field surrounding the human body. Although the faculty of auric or clairvoyant sight remains a comparatively rare phenomenon at this point in history, this aspect of the aura – the colours surrounding the living being – has nevertheless become a familiar phenomenon to many people over the last few years, especially since the advance in Kirlian photographic techniques, a special form of photography which uses extremely high-voltage cameras to provide a visual record of the energetic field around all living things.

There is, however, another aspect of the aura; and it was this aspect which alerted Vicky very soon to the realization that what had come through her was something more than mere beauty oils. The 'true aura' is an area of colour right at the centre of the body, around the size of a walnut, just above the navel and just inside. This area is perceived clairvoyantly to remain the same throughout a person's life, unlike the colours surrounding the body which change with altering states of physical health, emotions, and other factors. The true aura is like the thumbprint, expressing the particular hallmark of each individual, and communicating to those who are able to understand its language something of the fundamental nature of each soul.

The recognition of the true aura was to have enormous implications as *Aura-Soma* began to develop. Vicky noticed from the start that when a person felt especially attracted to one particular colour combination, the base fraction of that bottle nearly always bore a close correspondence to that person's central colour, their true aura. An encounter with

Balance, therefore, was very soon recognized as being much more than just a choosing of pretty colours. It was becoming clear that something happens in these encounters which is really very profound, and which led Vicky Wall to describe *Balance* as 'the mirror of the soul'. It seems that a meeting with *Balance* offers us the possibility of reaching the deepest aspects of our being; of accessing something of consciousness itself.

In any *Aura-Soma* workshop, as indeed in most consultations, this is the first and most arresting realization which students experience. For some, this recognition is instant, even if it is intangible. For me, numbed as I have said by whatever combination of forces, it came more slowly. Little by little, the bottles began to accompany me, in my mind, wherever I went: rather as one thinks constantly of a close friend. *Balance*, the heart of *Aura-Soma*; their quiet strength and their haunting, powerful beauty. A veil had been lifted from my eyes: there were few colours, surely, in the Western world to compare with these?

This was scarcely surprising since it was Vicky's deep knowledge of the natural methods of pharmacy used during the nineteenth century, learned directly from one of its practitioners with whom she worked during the last years of his life, and of the natural plant dyes imported directly through trade with India and other parts of the Far East, which gave these oils and waters their extraordinarily vibrant and luminescent colours.

Vicky's initial recognition of the connection between a person's true aura and the colour they chose formed the beginning of her understanding that colour is a universal language. This was a language which, together with Mike Booth, she intuited and researched for the rest of her life; and which Mike has continued to do ever since her death.

Thus the colour combinations contained within the *Balance* bottles represent, or speak, the universal language of colour.

This language, pertaining not to any one particular philosophy, or religion, or set of beliefs, shows us the way towards the core of ourselves and thus of humanity. The beauty of colour as a language is its very universality: just as it transcends the limitations of personality within an individual, so it transcends the divisions between different traditions of thought and belief. Colour offers us a path which moves away from divisiveness and towards unity, at a time when our very survival depends upon co-operation, true communication and mutual respect. A meeting with *Balance* provides us with a new opportunity: something may happen which goes deeper and wider than we have become accustomed to expect since languages first became divided. There is also much more contained within these bottles: this is to do with the way in which they are made and the energies which they contain.

Within each bottle is held a unique formula of energies from three kingdoms. The first of these is the plant kingdom. A bottle includes, in its top half, aromatic essential oils contained within other plant oils: these are coloured by natural plant dye of a very high quality. It is interesting to remember that while some of these dyes come from flowers and plants well known to Westerners, others come from plants of even more exotic hues which originate in the East. Thus even the physical constitution of the bottles is a mixture of natural ingredients from all over the world, reflecting on a material level the universality of their source. This oily mixture is perfectly balanced and resting upon the base fraction, which contains water of a very high purity with the addition of the watery herbal extracts of plants. These watery fractions are similarly coloured by means of natural plant dyes. *Aura-Soma*, from the very beginning, has drawn upon resources far and wide to incorporate into its physical base, as well as its philosophy, natural energies from all around the globe, which work together and in harmony.

The second category of energies contained within *Balance* is that of the mineral kingdom: that of crystals and gemstones. These vibrations enhance and finely tune the healing energies which are already present from the quality of the plants which each bottle contains.

The third category of energies is that portion of the animal kingdom which we call the hue-man one. Hue means colour, so in describing ourselves as human beings we could be said to be recognizing ourselves as beings of colour. The energies in *Balance* which come through those channels complete the trinity of energies which they contain. The healing energies which can come through plants and through the work of human beings are a normal and familiar part of our experience. For many people the energies of crystals and precious stones are less familiar and therefore less easily understood. Why should the addition of crystal and gem energy be so valuable to the effectiveness of *Balance*?

Minerals and gems, like plants, grow within the earth. Generally they grow deep down within the body of the earth. Everything that is part of the created world carries its signature: it gives us an indication of its quality by the colour or the sound which it emits; or by its shape. Gems and crystals are very deeply connected to colours, carrying energies whose waveforms correspond to the colours they display. Among many minerals, it is crystals and gems which have the purest and most beautiful crystallized molecular structure. They are solidified light; each family of crystals being the purest materialization of any one particular ray of light. They grow very slowly, deep within the bowels of the planet, absorbing over thousands of years the universal life force, while gradually growing and taking shape. Their energy is powerfully concentrated as well as very pure; and perhaps it contains, too, something extra. The lives of crystals stretch back into the deep past: why should they not bring with them into the present the crystallized wisdom of ancient times? Be that as it may, crystals have the ability to amplify energy, as demonstrated by their use in quartz watches: and this quality can be used to expand and concentrate the power of energy used for healing. On the night that *Balance* was born, Vicky Wall was given formulae by which she might transmit the precise quality of individual mineral energies to enhance and enrich the power which the bottles would contain.

The working of *Balance*, therefore, is multidimensional. Within each bottle we may find the combination of several different natural methods for restoring the balance of the system: herbal remedies, aromatic oils, crystals and gems. They also make the language of colours available to us in order that we may come to a very precise assessment of our being's needs of the moment. The colours we choose both reflect who we are and also provide us with the quality of energy which we need. When a client makes a selection of their four favourite colour combinations the consultant will be able to 'read' the information which the choice reveals. The choice offers insights about the past and the present; the challenges which the person faces and the gifts and strengths which they possess. The information throws light on the many different aspects of the person choosing the colours, from the spiritual and mental through the emotional and energetic or physical levels of their existence.

Once these aspects have been discussed, the therapist and client will choose one bottle from the selection as a therapeutic one. In practice this is nearly always the second bottle in the selection, though from time to time there may be reasons for choosing a different one. This means that the client will take the bottle twice every day – once in the morning and once in the evening – and shake it thoroughly so that the oily and watery ingredients form a temporary emulsion, which they will then massage on to the appropriate area of the skin. The shaking brings back together all the different aspects of the plants: the oil, the water and the colour. The skin is a semi-permeable membrane – which is why allopathic doctors administer certain slow-acting drugs by means of a plaster attached to the skin – from where they are gradually absorbed into the body. Thus when a small amount of emulsified *Balance* is applied as a massage balm to the appropriate area of the body, the combined energies of plants and minerals and colour itself are absorbed through the lymph system and the circulatory system to travel to the major glands and organs of the body, and then to repercuss on the aura, the energetic field which feeds the body with vital energy. The body has its own intelligence, so that in addition to our intuitive knowledge of the area to which the emulsion should be applied, the body will carry it to the region most in need of re-balancing, just in the same way that it carries the energy of an aspirin tablet either to the sore head or the broken ankle, depending upon the circumstance.

So, that unique 'something' contained within *Balance* has a physical base, and yet the source of its effectiveness, its real essence, is elusive. We need to look a little deeper at the way in which a selection of *Balance* bottles may be read and used, and to consider what we mean by balance. What, indeed, do we mean when we talk about 'healing' at all?

BALANCE

Once the implications of a selection of colours have been discussed, *Balance* is emulsified and then applied to the physical body. Yet the consequences of this action are likely to manifest on the other levels of our being: the emotional, the mental, the spiritual. This raises the important question of what we understand by healing. What is it that we are trying to heal?

The word 'heal' has the same root as 'whole', and even 'holy'. To be 'wholed' is to 're-member', or to bring together all the scattered members which comprise the many parts and levels of our being. It is to restore the free movement of energy which enables all those parts to work in harmony with one another. To be healed is to be 'wholed' or made whole, that the life force may flow smoothly, like a river proceeding steadily to its destination, through a being well-balanced on all levels. Well-being is Being well Balanced. In order for this to happen we need to remove the obstacles to the flow of this life force. Pain, stress, discomfort; any of these are what we experience when energy becomes stuck. Our primary task in healing ourselves, therefore, or in attempting to guide others towards finding their remedy, is to discover what it is that constitutes those obstacles to the free movement of energy.

Balance, and the language of colour, work together to give us that understanding. The blocks are like the chains or the prisons which we create for ourselves. The light of understanding which we can throw on our experiences dissolves those chains and offers us the space to move and grow.

The workshops begin with the study of colour: its nature and its symbolism. It is through *Balance* that this knowledge may then be grounded in a way which is useful for ourselves and for one another. How does this work? What is the system by which the gifts and strengths of a person may be so clearly seen? How is it that the difficulties and challenges which comprise the major issues of a person's life may be so precisely pinpointed? This is our primary focus as students on a workshop. It is what we are here to learn.

Each colour relates to a specific area of the body: the human being is seen, in colour terms, as a reflection of the rainbow. In other words the top of the rainbow, the Red, is reflected in the lowest area of the spine and below; the colours ascend through the body to the Violet at the crown, reflecting the colour seen at the bottom of the rainbow in the sky. If these colours correspond to specific areas of the body, which is the consensus of opinion given by all those with auric sight, then there must also be a correspondence with the other levels of our being: the emotions and thoughts, and the spirit. It is not by chance that novels for hundreds of years have, for example, told of men and women dying of a broken heart. The heart is the physical core of the emotions, just as the throat relates to communication. Indeed, as the experience of more than 14 years of *Aura-Soma* practice within workshops and individual consultations has shown, the correspondence of colour with differing states of mind, heart and spirit has the accuracy of a laser beam.

So it is that little by little *Aura-Soma* has moved away, as it has evolved, from the definition of itself as a healing system and towards the idea that this is really a means by which we may modify our consciousness. The process of modifying our consciousness may be, and indeed often is, followed by a re-balancing on the physical as well as other levels. Nevertheless, healing is much more complex and profound than the curing of physical symptoms or the offering of a box of tissues to one in tears. When Vicky Wall used to teach years ago that any attempt to re-balance the physical body without regard to the aura could only be temporary and that the imbalance would surely return, she was recognizing the much deeper level on which true healing must take effect. True healing brings the light of understanding to a situation, so that whatever it is that we are facing we may move towards it in faith and trust and peace.

This is the real purpose of *Balance*. Let us look in a little more detail at the process of choosing and interpreting a selection of colour combinations.

A CONSULTATION

There are currently 98 *Balance* bottles in the range, each one containing equal fractions of oils resting on herbal waters. In most cases the oily fraction is of a different colour from the watery one, in some they are the same; it is always clear that they are divided. When we come to look at this selection, which is displayed in a well-lit position where the glowing living energies may thrive and radiate their message, we are invited, initially, to choose our single favourite combination. Our choice may surprise us: it may bear no apparent relation to the colours which we normally choose in our clothing and our cushions. Nevertheless, if we open ourselves to follow our instinct our selection will be true.

For some this initial choice is immediate. Others may at first feel a little overwhelmed; unsure of which one to reach for. If there is difficulty in finding certainty it might help to imagine that this will be the last occasion on which we may choose a bottle, and that we shall have to live with it for the rest of our life, as though we were about to depart for a desert island. Which then, out of all these possibilities, would feel the most comfortable?

The first clue relates to the phenomenon already observed, the correlation of the base colour with the colour of the true aura. In recognizing our true colour or colours we are recognizing something about the deepest essence of ourselves. The base fraction of the first bottle shows something about our fundamental nature; the top fraction indicates something of the path which we have chosen in this life. This path will not only enable us to express our natural quality; it will also provide obstacles. Like the obstacles in an assault course, they are an in-built part of the set-up. They were there from the beginning. It is in surmounting those obstacles that we may hope to learn our lessons and find strength.

If we bring the particular quality or qualities with which we are endowed into the circumstances of our lives, learning our lessons and endeavouring, through our experience, to grow, then we may become the most of which we are capable. Thus, if we look at the *combination* of the two fractions of this first bottle, the quality and the life path, we can see a picture of our fullest potential. All this means that this first choice of bottle is highly significant: through it we can glean the soul purpose of the person whose choice it is. It may show us what is the nature of their 'mission': that is to say, what it was that they came into this life to do, or find, or be. So, while the first bottle thus indicates much about our quality and strengths, it also points up possible areas of struggle in the life path. The second bottle highlights those areas of struggle which have provided the greatest challenge.

To choose a second bottle, it is recommended that we repeat the procedure for the first: we imagine that we have only one choice. This accomplished, we continue to a third and finally to a fourth combination. The second bottle, then, pinpoints the major difficulties of the past; but it also shows the potential within them for the greatest learning. It is therefore known as the Challenge and the Gift. The upper fraction shows predominantly those issues of which we already have a degree of awareness; whereas the lower one tends to indicate those of which we are largely unconscious.

The third choice of bottle talks about the present situation. How are we coping with it all now? Have we dealt with a good bit of it, or are we going round and round in circles with the same old stuff? Again the top represents, by and large, the conscious; the base shines its light on the the issues of which we are largely unaware.

The fourth bottle indicates the general direction in which we are heading. By whatever it is that we are investing our energy in at this moment, and the way we are investing it, we create the quality of the next moment. Thus, again, our unconscious mind knows roughly what we are up to and will give us some clear suggestions about the way we are going.

These are the guidelines. Ultimately, the *Balance* bottles are keys which unlock our intuition; but these are the foundation stones of the structure which we learn, and within which we work. As students on a workshop, we may find that energies move fast. The combined effects of a number of people opening together to the movement of energy and the softening of blockages creates an atmosphere in which mountains may be moved.

In order to understand clearly the process of what happens when we are faced with a selection of four *Balance* bottles, we need to see the colours as the real choices of living people. A sample case taken from another workshop will illustrate

something of these general principles, before we embark on a
journey to explore the language of colour.

Rosemary

Rosemary, the name by which we shall know her, was in her
late thirties when she attended her first *Aura-Soma* course.
Although she was a gifted astrologer, she only practised this
from time to time. More significant than this was Rosemary's
musical talent. Since early childhood, music had been the
abiding passion of her life, and she had progressed in early
childhood to the level of competence very rarely attained
even by those two or three times her age. Yet for years she had
been unable to play. Her musical energy was totally blocked,
so that for several years she had given up even trying. Any
attempt to play the cello, she had found during these years,
simply brought up an apparently endless fountain of tears.
Bored with the tears and the heaviness of the grief she seemed
to carry with her, she had put away the cello in a cupboard.
It was if the whole of her musical life had been put away
under lock and key. With these rare gifts both as an
astrological counsellor and a musician locked up, as it were, in
the deep freeze, she earned her living by doing menial tasks as
a temporary secretary. This enabled her to survive, but not to
live.

Rosemary was an unusual student: powerful, passionate,
intense. She had an acute intellect which was always on the
alert; and a rare depth of vision. The consequence of this was
that for some years she had worked hard on herself in an
attempt to gain the knowledge and the insight which would
enable her to dissolve this paralysing block. Nevertheless,
this was a labyrinth which she had never yet found a way
through.

On the day that she asked to share her choice with the
group, her bottles ran like this:

45	52	76	59
<u>Turquoise</u>	<u>Pale Pink</u>	<u>Pink</u>	<u>Pale Yellow</u>
Magenta	Pale Pink	Gold	Pale Pink

The Magenta in the base of the first bottle showed Rosemary's blend of passion and tenderness; her deep commitment to people and to her purpose. This purpose, the Turquoise suggested, was primarily the creative communication of the heart through some kind of artistic endeavour. The Magenta also suggested something of a tendency towards self-sacrifice. The Turquoise indicated a strong love of freedom, a sense of responsibility, and a powerful creative gift. The bottle confirmed Rosemary's profound love of her art and her ability to communicate, through music, a quality of energy which could heal and uplift. So what was the problem?

Here we refer, in particular, to the second bottle. What we see is the very palest Pink. In *Aura-Soma* we see the paler colours as more, not less, intense. They are the colours with the light shone through. They may show intense awareness and also intense suffering. Pink refers to the feminine intuitive mothering energy; to unconditional love. In second place we are looking at a problem. Pink is most likely to be related to the mother: it could indicate either smothering or neglect.

Here it indicated both. Rosemary's mother had been a talented young opera singer when she married and found herself before long with a couple of children. She had a volatile nature and a passion to perform. The centre of the stage was her natural home. Frustration was already running high, and the marriage on the rocks, when Rosemary arrived in the world. Before long the mother resorted to barbiturates and alcohol and rapidly lost the frail remnants of her mental balance. There was time only for the parents to produce one further child before Rosemary's father departed under the strain, leaving his young daughter to cope with looking after her mother and baby sister. The older sisters, like Rosemary's father, abandoned the scene as soon as they were able. Thus Rosemary's early life was a drama against which Cinderella herself could not have attempted to compete. All day, apart from those hours when she escaped to school, Rosemary scrubbed and cooked, hounded by a whip if ever she slacked. At night her sleep was broken by the constant demands of her stoned and drunken mother. She escaped when she dared, to play her cello; but never for long: as Rosemary's rare talent became more and more apparent, her mother confiscated her cello and locked it in a cupboard and hid the key. Rosemary searched the house, and found the key, only for this extraordinary scene to be many times repeated, until finally her spirit all but broke, and she gave up the attempt.

It was small wonder that, even in her thirties, Rosemary was unable to make music. Nor was it surprising that she harboured intense resentment, frustration and rage, which was also apparent from the second bottle. How was she doing with all this in the present? The third bottle, the Pink over Gold, echoed the everlasting love which without terms or conditions she offered to those she knew. With so much Pink throughout the selection, it was also clear that Rosemary had a deep and unsatisfied need for love for herself: 'I need to be loved as I am, not as you want me to be', was the message that resounded throughout. The Gold in the base showed a well of deep irrational fear: the kind of fear which cannot be lulled by an effort of reason or will. It also showed that Rosemary was prepared to access her deep intuitive wisdom and compassion, that through love and understanding she could learn to forgive. Each bottle has a name: the name of this one is 'Trust'.

Rosemary's fourth and final bottle, like her second, was pale and intense, containing yet again the Pink, and the Yellow which is not dissimilar to the Gold. It was as if the third bottle was turned upside down and brought into the light, so that the learning could be gathered up and used. The Yellow, which had indicated fear, would soon be brought to the conscious mind and transmuted to knowledge and wisdom. The Pink was still there in the depths: behind it and underneath it all was a bottomless well of love which she might soon learn to offer to herself. 'Love is letting go of fear.' The bottles, with their fresh colours of spring, contained a powerful promise of rebirth.

This is merely the palest outline of the portrait which the bottles drew. The average consultation lasts for around 45 minutes. Nevertheless, it illustrates something of the principles involved. The language of colour, while in one way remarkably simple and direct, is simultaneously complex and profound. There are relationships between the colours; the energies of colours are combined and concealed in different ways; the missing colours are often as significant as those which are chosen. To learn to understand what a selection of bottles is telling us takes training and practice. Eventually the techniques of interpretation and the essence of the colours become as familiar and instinctive as, say, the controls on a car and the feeling for the roads and the surroundings. Then the bottles become, for the trained therapist, keys which unlock the doors to our intuition, and healing energy can flow with a penetrating power. This energy is like water: water, on the one hand, has the force to burst dams, and the gentleness, on the other hand, to support life in the womb; and it is the penetrating power of water which holds everything together. Without it all would be dust. The healing energies of light flow in the same way: powerful, penetrating and infinitely gentle.

The healing which Rosemary received on that workshop initiated a process of change in her which set her on the road towards a greater freedom than she had ever known. Such change does not often come easily or swiftly. Nevertheless,

Rosemary's cello has emerged from its cupboard. She knows now with certainty that her primary purpose in this life is to make music. She is well aware of the work still to be done, but her music is beginning once more to come alive.

The colours address us at a deeper level than merely what has been created by circumstance. What kinds of things might it be that this language of colours may teach us which can have such a radical effect on our well-being? To understand the answer to this, we need to set out on a journey upwards through the energy stations of the body: a journey through the rainbow, and – maybe? – over to the other side.

THE ADVENTURE

Plate 6 is an artist's impression of the way in which Vicky Wall perceived man in his perfect state. It represents, if you like, her vision of the future: the rainbow being that we might become in a state of perfect balance and harmony at all levels of our being. As you look at it, you may imagine that what you see represents a picture of yourself. In reality none of us is — as yet — so well adjusted. Yet this model represents the balance which would bring us peace of mind and heart, body and spirit.

At this time when there is so much opening up around the field of our health and our growth many people have become aware that what we can perceive with the five senses is merely the beginning; that there is much more beyond. Colour is the visible part of the whole of the spectrum of light: the safe part of the spectrum which relates to us as physical organisms. The vibrations of colour which are visible to the human eye and safe for the organism are those which exist between the infra-red at one end and the ultra-violet at the other. It is these vibrations which are harnessed with the *Balance* bottles and the rest of the *Aura-Soma* system. Yet ironically when working with colour we are accessing healing energies which themselves are not necessarily visible.

'What is healing energy?', people ask from time to time. 'I can't see it. How can I know it is real?'

Yet nor can we see the energy of electricity, or magnetism, or gravity, or the wind. We can only feel it, and see its effects. Similarly, at this point in the history of the Western world, most of us cannot see auras, the energetic fields which surround the bodies of all living things; or chakras, the energy stations which occur at intervals down the spines of all living creatures. If we want visual confirmation that an energy field surrounds a living body, we rely on the evidence of Kirlian photographs which provide a visual record of at least some of these energies. Yet many people, with a reasonable level of training, are able to feel auras; and everyone may benefit from the effects of their being re-balanced, whether or not they actually feel the energies as they receive them. Clairvoyant means, simply, clear seeing: in Vicky's youth this was a rare phenomenon, and while it remains comparatively so at present there are, nevertheless, increasing numbers of people opening up to these finer senses.

The normally invisible aspects of the energies of colour are not measurable. We are looking, really, at the subtle realms of human anatomy, and in this field there are no objective criteria. We are largely dependent, apart from our own experience and intuition, and the limited information provided by Kirlian photography, on the evidence of those gifted with clairvoyant sight; and even in this the details observed by one person do not necessarily tally precisely with those of another.

This is where we have to open up to the receptive intuitive part of ourselves, as well as to those who are prepared to share their knowledge. Such knowledge has been available in the East for thousands of years. Here, perhaps more than in the study of any other aspect of human health or consciousness, there is no possibility of a 'control', in the scientific sense.

Human beings in any case, by their very nature, are not subject to scientific study by anyone who recognizes one essential fact: that by virtue of being human, each one of us is unique. The variations between auras and the subtle flowing changes within them are limitless.

There is among clairvoyants, however, and in the traditional literature, a reasonably broad base of agreement regarding the larger picture. We therefore have a model of the human light body – the human being expressed in light – which seems to work. This really is the limit of what concerns me in this book. What I hope to convey is largely experience rather than theory.

THE CHAKRAS

According to ancient Hindu traditions every human being has seven chakras, or energy stations, in and around the body: these are reservoirs and generators of energy. They correspond to the colours of the rainbow, and it is through these chakras that the universal life force enters and feeds us. Each of these stations oscillates at a different frequency and responds to different vibrations of light, or in other words has its own colour. Individual colours are produced by different wavelengths of light. The chakras are located from the base of the spine to the crown, and therefore connect the energy system of the body top to bottom.

To understand the necessity for keeping the chakras well adjusted, Vicky Wall suggested the analogy of seven television sets stacked on top of one another. In order to obtain the clearest reception, it is necessary to keep each set finely tuned. If we do that, allowing energy to flow freely and smoothly, we will see a better picture and hear a clearer sound. Another helpful comparison is with the strings of a guitar. If each string is properly tuned then they can work together to produce a sound which is harmonious. If even one string is a little out of tune, the whole of the flow of the music will be affected. So it is with the chakras: each one is intimately connected to all the others, and thus the imbalance of one will affect the whole of the energetic system of the body.

While the Hindu tradition has for many centuries described the chakras as spinning wheels of energy, Vicky Wall saw the subtle energy system a little differently. She preferred to use the term 'energy station' rather than 'chakra', as she saw the different zones as bands of colour which surrounded the entire body. This, therefore, is the model with which we work in *Aura-Soma*.

The rainbow being in perfect balance will have each aspect of the full spectrum perfectly poised, in a state of equilibrium between those above and those below. Such a being in perfect balance will allow energy to travel freely through all the channels connecting above with below and the inner with the outer. The understanding of the chakras and the language of colour, and the experience of colour and light, can lead us into an exciting journey. For some this is experienced as a journey from relative darkness into light; from confusion into clarity. We could go further and suggest that the journey can become an adventure. Through colour we can pioneer our way into country which has scarcely been explored. Even in our conscious lives the territory we tread is often unknown: the unconscious is a positive wilderness. If we are equipped with signposts and a map we can see more of the possibilities: the main roads, the places of interest and beauty as well as the pitfalls and the dirt tracks.

At the very beginning, God created the light. The void of darkness contained the infinity of potential. Out of that void, the potential, came that primal force, the energy of light, and from there came colour. Each of us, at our very beginning, emerges from the darkness; the full potential contained, from the very start, within the thought, and then within the single cell combining all that we might inherit from the past: from the line of our father and the line of our mother. That single cell will expand and bloom, emerging from the darkness into light and colour. This is a journey which I believe we make many many times, the soul returning to the source only to emerge once more and land on earth, little by little to find illumination. The journey becomes an adventure, a treasure hunt, as we seek the clues and find the rewards. It is a journey which may be repeated many times in a lifetime, as the circumstances which we live present us with opportunities for new discoveries. And maybe also, ultimately, spread over the course of many lifetimes, the adventure continues for thousands of years. This, again, is where mankind may benefit from signposts and a map.

Rudolf Steiner was one of the first pioneers into colour not merely as an outer reality with physical properties but as a subjective reality: the question of how it is that as individuals we actually receive and experience colour. It was his recognition of the effect of colour on every phase of the individual's life which led Steiner to develop a system of education and a way of life based on colour and rhythm. Steiner saw White as the image of the spirit, and Black as the image of lifelessness; and he saw colour as the borderland between light and darkness. In other words he believed that colour is created when light shines into the darkness.

This is fascinating when we begin to look at the possibility of the evolution of our consciousness through the awareness of colour. Colour can be seen, according to Steiner's borderland, as a bridge between earthly consciousness and our higher perception, between our material concerns and our spiritual nature. Where these two are not balanced and in harmony sickness arises, and sickness is often accompanied by a sense of darkness and depression. This is literally true: Kirlian photographs of the auras of people suffering some type of sickness show patches of darkness where there are energy blockages, which is another way of saying where there is illness. True healing, therefore, must involve the re-establishing and rebalancing of light around the person's aura.

Let us consider another image: the pure White light may be seen as the mother/father, or the Master of all the colours which emanate from it. Seen in this way the colours are the children of White light. As hue-man beings therefore, beings of colour, we might see ourselves as children of the White light, every one unique in the particular way in which we receive and transform the light. As we explore and grow, we experiment with different possibilities and identities; we move through experience after experience in the process of coming into our own truth.

Living in this earthly dimension, as 'children', in the borderland of colour between light and darkness, we learn and grow and evolve. Our lives involve constant interplay between forces which are complementary and opposite: life and death, light and darkness, male and female, passion and discipline; each one incomplete without the balance of its complement. Over-concern with the preoccupations of material life will cause the spirit to wilt and starve; an over-absorption in the world of spirit may prevent us from taking firm root in the material world. Our aim is to achieve balance, but balance at a deeper level than we ever could have achieved without the difficulties which initially caused us to become unbalanced. Through the raising of our awareness we may achieve a greater degree of balance than was there when the journey began.

Sickness, dis-ease, may thus have the function of helping us towards true healing: by bringing our attention, through discomfort or pain, to aspects of ourselves which are out of balance, it shines the light on areas of darkness, prodding us awake in order that we may rediscover ourselves at a new level. In this journey through the borderland between light and darkness we have moments of great illumination: moments, for example, of deep insight, tenderness, inspiration or ecstasy. At other times we move downwards towards the darkness, the shadow: towards depression, greed, or anger, for example. Both these states are likely to be reflected in the colours which we choose, and in their varying hues.

To live too much in the shadow may indicate negativity and fear. Our tendency is to be negative: seen in simple gravitational terms, it is easier to slide downwards than to climb upwards. Yet the possibility, and our right as human beings, is to overcome the downward trend and to move upwards towards that which is positive. Our colour choices can provide us with insights into the aspects of our journey which particularly require our positive attention at the moment. The challenge throughout the journey of life is to attempt to remain on the positive side of the energies which surround us.

Each chakra may be seen as a stage in a journey which we make through the process of life. Our colour choices, with their combinations and their hues and tints, and their positions, have much to show us about where we are on the path. The adventure begins with our arrival on earth through the first chakra, the Red one, and the progression is then upwards through the remaining chakras until we reach the top chakras, the Violet and beyond that the Magenta which reconnect us with Heaven. At every stage in the adventure there are challenges, hurdles which will test our spiritual muscle and staying power. Every stage also carries its joys and rewards, which are the greater for the lessons learned. Think of the joy of the young child who finally overcomes the limitations of life on hands and knees and finds her feet.

This adventure, which is represented in the ascending energy centres is one which, as individuals, we experience to one extent or another in each lifetime; and perhaps, as already suggested, many times over in a lifetime, as well as in many lives throughout the evolution of each individual soul. The journey can be looked at also in a wider context, and this is perhaps an even more exciting challenge as we move into a new time, leaving behind us the Age of Pisces and treading the dawn of the Age of Aquarius. As history proceeds, mankind as a whole can be seen to be making this journey through the energetic stations. This is a voyage which offers the possibility of ever-ascending consciousness and ever-expanding quality, as a race, as well as in our individual lives.

Man and woman are unique in the whole of the animal kingdom: we are the only creatures who stand upright in the world, all chakras exposed to the light. Like the six-pointed star, our heads reach upwards towards Heaven while our feet remain on earth. Firmly grounded, we may yet focus on the Heaven energy which descends from above to keep us clear. As we work towards ever-ascending consciousness we may achieve true balance: head in Heaven, feet on earth, centre flowing free.

Every colour, and therefore every chakra, contains messages. Each colour contains information at many different levels: spiritual, mental, emotional and energetic, or physical. Some of this information is about gifts and strengths; some is about difficulties and lessons. As long as each chakra remains in an unawakened state we are likely to be limited to a certain extent by the constraints and difficulties which that chakra contains. As the light of understanding increases so does the possibility of overcoming these constraints and discovering the gifts contained within the experience.

The third chakra, for example, has to do with the individual will, with achievement, with power and its use or mis-use. It relates to the colour Yellow. Difficulties within this energy centre may include either an over-inflated ego, with its accompanying sense of greed and search for the control of others; or, on the other hand, a sense of unworthiness which prevents us from developing our individuality. As the light of awareness is shone into this solar plexus, the sun centre of our being, we may find intense self-knowledge and perception; this in turn may lead to a genuine sense of self-worth which leads to the flowering of our individuality and happiness.

As a colour moves from the hue towards the lighter tones it becomes a tint; it is moving nearer to the White light. As it moves towards the darker tones it becomes a shade. The challenge for every one of us is to remain on the positive side of each colour. *Balance* contains very few shades and many tints, since the intention in *Aura-Soma* is to work consciously with the energies of light. This is not to deny the shadow side. It is rather to acknowledge that the light is always stronger than the darkness; that in giving energy to the light we can further enhance its power.

It is, however, vital to understand that colour offers no evaluation or judgement. Colour in itself is neutral: each ray is a different aspect of pure White light, each absolutely necessary to the totality of that light. Similarly, whether the colour chosen is a hue, a shade or a tint is simply a matter of analysis. It is a reflection of whatever is the current state of affairs within the person choosing the colours, with either their hues or shades or tints. Someone may choose four of the palest possible tints: this may well indicate that the person has a fairly acute spiritual awareness. It may also show that, perhaps, they suffer a lot of pain on one or another level; and maybe that they find it difficult to ground their awareness in physical life. They may, for example, be very absent-minded and disorganized. Colour provides a mirror, not an appraisal.

Everything has its polar opposite. If light is the opposite of darkness, love is the opposite of fear. Gerald Jampolsky's well-known phrase, 'Love is letting go of fear', acknowledges the existence of these two polar energies: love and fear. Both exist in all of us. Everything which does not come from love comes from fear. If love comes from light it follows that fear comes from darkness. The movement downwards towards darkness and negativity is a manifestation of fear. Every movement upwards is a movement towards the light, which must be a move towards love, overcoming the negativity of fear. Our choice of colours helps to reveal those areas where the fear impedes our movement and progress.

This is all very well, but what can we do about it?

We can, first, look at our choice of colours. Colour holds the key to many doors. Then we can open ourselves to the insights which those colours offer. Next we can co-operate with the colour, applying it to our bodies, and contemplating the lessons it has to teach us. Before we can let go of fear we must, surely, learn to befriend it and understand it. Perhaps once we see something of what it is we can open up a communication with it and listen to the answers which it may provide. What, after all, is the darkness? It is the shadow; it is ignorance, or what we choose to ignore and suppress. As we shine more and more light on those aspects of ourselves which we find the most difficult to accept and understand, we move nearer and nearer to that light, or perhaps to en-light-enment. Thus we may put roots into the darkness, nurturing all that it contains and bringing it to the light. By accepting that which we would reject and acknowledging that which we would keep from ourselves, we can harness the energies of love in order to create beauty and order out of the apparent fragments and difficulties of our lives. This buried 'stuff', once processed and brought to the light, may be transmuted and transformed. Just as the darkness of the soil produces fruits and flowers, heavenly scents and textures and tastes and sights and sounds, so can we transform our experience and our understanding: to paintings, myths and poems and stories, letters, dances, songs; to foods prepared with love which nurture ourselves and others with a healing vibration. Or it may express itself simply as a smile, as tenderness bestowed on ourselves or on a loved one as we begin to accept that the universe, and our part in it, is fundamentally benign.

CHAPTER 6

RED

The process begins with the colour Red. Red is about energy, and our link with the earth. Energy is the first priority for physical life. Red is the energy to love and the energy to live. Red is the earth mother, the life blood of the world. It holds our feet upon the ground; it allows the material energy of incarnation to enter the body and give it life. It is the anchoring of spirit to the body, the earthing of our ideas and intentions. Plate 6 shows that the Red energy station covers the area from the pubic bone and the base of the spine right down to the feet; and it includes the hands. Through our hands and feet the Red connects us with the energy of the earth: it tunes our own energy field into the ley line energetic system of the earth, supplying us with life, with positive and negative power. The Red energy enables us, through the actions of our hands and our feet, to materialize our thoughts, our emotions and even our will.

Red is the first, or the base, chakra. This is where the journey begins. Red has to do with our first experience of physical life. The process of birth is a Red experience. Whether we travel through the birth canal or whether we are delivered by Caesarean section, we arrive in this world through the Red area of the body.

What is the nature of that experience? We have lived for some months in the comfort and warmth of the mother's body, floating around in a nice warm bath, all basic needs met with no real effort required on our part. Then comes the moment of birth; the severing of the umbilical cord and our first encounter with the element of air, with changes of temperature, and soon with hunger. We must learn to breathe, to suck and later to chew. We must learn, in fact, to survive. We emerge, all unsuspecting, from nine months of peace, quiet and warmth in the soft dark intimacy of the innermost recesses of our mother, to glaring lights and a most precarious sense of balance. We are dangled, as likely as not, by our feet to receive a hefty slap on the back.

How may we respond to this somewhat sudden set of challenges? Are we going to scream in righteous indignation as the doctor hits us, demanding in return for our discomfort that at least the world out there owes us our basic requirements for survival? Will we therefore go out to meet those challenges with aggression, or might we retire into fear and neurosis, unable to ask directly for whatever it is that we need?

How we react to this initial experience, whether we scream for attention to make sure nothing gets forgotten or whether we retreat in fear and eventually into neurosis, lays down the pattern for our life. From that first moment onwards, our personality will lean towards one or the other of these tendencies. The challenge through our lives is to achieve balance: to move too far in either direction is to move away from balance and towards disharmony.

The base chakra is the bottom line. The bottom line, in human experience, is survival, and meeting those needs for our survival: food, shelter and warmth. The Red Cross carries the promise that we will be helped to survive.

After our personal survival comes the larger matter of the survival of the species, and hence reproduction. Red is thus linked also to that important part of the primal energy, the sexual drive. Red lipstick, and the Red lips which feature in many advertisements, are an obvious use of the Red energy to stimulate the base chakra. The suitor who offers Red roses is using another familiar symbol of the Red energy.

Physically the Red area relates to the adrenal glands, the glands whose function is closely associated with the issue of survival; it is adrenalin which stimulates our response to an emergency: 'fight or flight'.

Red indicates a practical person with their feet on the ground. It may be chosen by people with a lot of drive and ambition. People are drawn to Red who enjoy the physical challenge and experience of being on earth.

Energy, and survival. Without the basic energy for life even the survival needs will not be met. The choice of a lot of Red in a selection may indicate an energetic person, or someone who is an energizer for others or, conversely, someone in need of energy and drive. It is an energizer, a colour which stimulates and goads us into action.

Red is our own life blood. The Red blood carries oxygen through the veins, keeping us from moment to moment alive on this earth. It circulates nourishment to all the cells of our bodies. The Red blood is the blood of brotherhood and solidarity: family ties and political passion. Chairman Mao's 'Little Red Book'; 'Reds under the bed': these are (or were) phrases which referred to a political ideology which is, paradoxically, fundamentally materialistic, and Red is the colour above all the others which is associated with the material world.

Like all the other colours, in itself Red is neutral: it simply reflects how things are. Nor does any one colour have any greater intrinsic worth than any other. Every colour is an aspect of the full spectrum of White light. All colours have some attributes which are positive and some attributes which present themselves as challenges, and the task in our attempt to evolve is to remain on the positive side of the energy.

Red is the slowest of all the wavelengths within the visible spectrum, and yet it is also the most stimulating. It is one of the safest colours for cars because the eyes register its presence earlier than they register the less stimulating colours.

Colour, the visible part of the electromagnetic spectrum, is the safe part of that spectrum. Next to Red comes Infra-Red and then the frequency becomes that of electricity. Red is therefore the closest of all the colours to this form of energy: very powerful, dynamic and physical in its impact. Its wavelength is long and slow, but it moves with the strength of an ocean wave: hence its power. Hence too, perhaps, the association of Red with danger. 'Red Alert' spells danger. A Red traffic light warns us to stop or risk our very survival. The energy of Red contains a warning for caution and maybe for moderation. If this were carried to extremes it might indicate rigidness or stubbornness; an unwillingness to take on new experiences: maybe a 'stick-in-the-mud', someone who is stuck in the earth to such an extent that they cannot see the way forward. In its healthy, free-flowing state, however, Red is an energy of movement and progress: the Red motivates us to go out and achieve. It is an energy of courage and daring; even sometimes of revolution.

Red is also the warmest end of the spectrum, the colour of Red-hot metal and embers. It can keep us warm and vibrant or it can burn us to death. Red is the physical heat of a fire and it is the emotional heat of our passion. It is the mental heat of concentration and the spiritual heat of commitment and sacrifice. The Red energy, through pleasure or perhaps through pain, wakes us up. It is an energy which tends to make us react. If we touch a piece of hot metal our body will react in indignation, in order to preserve itself. On a deeper level maybe an experience, perhaps of surprise or shock, will promote a reaction at that level, stimulating us to wake up to ourselves.

Red also has to do with passion. Passion can manifest as an emotional and physical energy; or spiritually as the energy demonstrated by Christ. *Aura-Soma* associates the Red energy with Christ because the Red carries within it the potential for many of the qualities which Christ displayed so powerfully: love and passion and commitment; courage and strength; righteous anger and the energy for change. Thus the Red energy contains the potential for us to awaken to those qualities within ourselves: the possibility of our awakening to the new being within us, bringing awareness, consciousness, and the grounding of these. It is when we ground these qualities that they become more than just an idea and we become responsible.

The Red energy is primarily the masculine aspect of ourselves: dynamic, outgoing, dominant.

Red is the energy of love in its many forms. It is the colour of heat and fire and Red roses and carnations. In varying stages of its hue Red can be passion, deep commitment, the love which is possessive and conditional or the love which expresses itself in self-sacrifice. It is also the colour of anger and frustration and resentment. It is finely balanced. It can provide the body with healing, vitality and strength. It can surround the body in love, passion and endearment but it can destroy the body with anger, hatred and fear. It can move us forward or it can hold us back, perhaps manifesting physically as inflammation, irritation, or cramps. It is the colour which gives life and it is the colour which takes life away.

The challenge is to remain positive. Therefore what, for example, are the possibilities for expressing the energy of anger? Christ displayed a righteous anger in the turning of the money lenders' tables: this is the anger which rights wrongs and injustices; an anger displayed by Robin Hood when he robbed the rich to feed the poor. This is the Red energy in a healthy and free-flowing state; an anger which can be creative. What about the expression of our own personal anger: our frustrations and resentments? Do we manifest these in a creative way? Or do we suppress the anger, allowing it to fester and express itself indirectly? Do we turn it in towards ourselves so that it manifests as some physical or emotional symptom, such as headaches, arthritis or depression? Or do we recognize it for what it is: an energy, which may be used for our growth and empowerment? The challenge in the Red, once we have begun to overcome the fundamental anxiety around survival, is to learn to work with anger rather than against it, recognizing it and expressing it constructively in order that its energy may be harnessed and used in a positive way. Its powerful force may be transmuted and used to develop qualities such as concentration, persistence, tenderness, protectiveness, or courage.

Survival issues and the creative expression of anger, resentment and frustration, therefore, are major challenges at the very beginning of the journey. The more thoroughly we overcome these difficulties, the better equipped we shall be to enjoy the adventures to come, and find fulfilment.

The Red energy can be one of enormous enthusiasm, of commitment and drive which moves us to invest energy and passion in whatever we value and believe in. It can motivate us to succeed on the material plane. It can inspire us to connect with passion, determination, and commitment, so that we live our lives to the full. Conversely, if we are caught up in anger and frustration, perhaps the Red indicates a lack of energy rather than an abundance of it, and a need to look at what it is that is preventing its healthy flow.

The Red ray is the blood of the planet. Hippocrates and other early physicians believed that the life force was carried in the blood. It was this belief which gave rise to the idea of the 'sanguine' personality: those with the 'sang', the life blood of energy and optimism flowing through their veins. In its highest form it can lend strength to spirit, producing sublime energy and vitality. In its lowest form it can indicate extreme discontent, draining a body of life.

So we have a picture of the essence of the Red energy; we have images and symbols which combine to give us an overall idea of the quality of Red, with its challenges and its gifts. Let's look at some stories to illustrate how these symbols and ideas can help us to see the picture when a client makes a selection. These pinpoint the issues pertaining specifically to the Red energy, and show how that Red energy can work in action, when the appropriate *Balance* bottle is brought to remedy a situation. With 98 *Balance* bottles currently in the range, there are obviously a considerable number which contain Red in combination with other colours. Rather than examine these combinations, we shall confine ourselves to looking at a fairly clear and undiluted Red theme, which thus addresses most specifically the Red issues.

Anna

Bottle No. 6: Red/Red, the Energy Bottle, is specifically a re-energizer, helping us to connect with the basic energy and enthusiasm for life and for love. It helps us to get our feet on the ground. It enables us to find vitality and courage. It aids us in finding a sense of responsibility, especially in relation to managing the material side of life. It can ease muscle cramps and other problems related to circulation.

Anna was a woman in her late thirties who came for a consultation because she was suffering from deep fatigue and listlessness to the point where she was having difficulty in managing a full day's work in the graphics department of an advertising company. She was also suffering severely from the cold, and from muscle cramps in her lower legs.

By the time Anna turned to *Aura-Soma* the problem had been chronic for several months. Her doctor had discovered no physical explanation for her condition, and had recommended a holiday and plenty of rest. She had taken herself to Spain for a fortnight and come home to find herself soon as weary as before.

The Red/Red bottle came up in second place. Within the selection there was also a certain proportion of Pink, Orange and Yellow, but the emphasis was heavily on the Red energy. We examined the issues around this colour. What were the frustrations and resentments in Anna's life? She was clearly talented and very capable, but the Red energy was evidently, for some reason, blocked.

Anna lived with her elderly mother, with whom she had had a fraught relationship since her early childhood. Her father had died some years previously, and since her widowhood in late middle age her mother, Sybil, had turned to Anna for physical, material and emotional support. Sybil herself had retired into a comfortable routine of invalidity, with a large range of pills, confident in the knowledge that her daughter would provide and cope.

Anna was the only child of the marriage, her mother's last hope in her early forties after a chain of miscarriages; thus the pressure had been on her from the start. This had initially taken the form of 'smother love', until Anna was in her teens when the mother had attempted increasingly to mould and control her. Anna, with her passionate, slightly wild nature and her love of art, had no desire to spend her life as a secretary and a cook catering to her mother's needs. But her childhood had consisted of a ceaseless reminder of her great good fortune in being here, her mother having survived her birth and a subsequent haemorrhage only by the skill of the attendant medical staff.

This was a clear example of someone who, from the

beginning, had received love which was highly conditional. Anna's father had been affectionate and kind but had tended to take a back seat in the face of the mother's obvious dominance. The tenuous hold we have on our survival had also been clearly conveyed to her from the start. Anna had found it hard, too, to connect with her own innate feminine quality; so she had tended to compensate by being outgoing and dominant in the world outside her home. The search for real love had never been satisfied, and she had made do with a series of incomplete sexual relationships, generally conducted away from home and with the disapproval of her mother.

Anna was, naturally, angry: she was resentful of her mother's demands; she was frustrated by the limitations imposed upon her; and she was tired. The Red energy which might serve her so well had been turned inwards, leaving her feeling depressed and helpless.

Previously unaware of the feeling of guilt which had for so long locked her into this unproductive relationship, Anna soon began to recognize that this state of affairs helped her mother no more than it did her. As we discussed the picture which the bottles had revealed, she saw that the best way in which she could support her mother was in paying attention to her own needs first. Only then would she find the strength to do what was necessary.

Anna began working with the Red/Red bottle, applying it every morning around her hips and on the soles of the feet. She also massaged it into the areas of her legs which suffered attacks of cramp. She was advised to avoid using it later in the day, since its energizing effects are likely to keep one awake; and sleep at this time would be an important part of her remedy.

It was three months before Anna came for another consultation. Her energy was radically changed: she was no longer tired, she was enthusiastic about her life and her work;

and she had arranged to move to her own house, in the same town, but at a distance from her mother, whom she now saw only every few days. Though she still felt the cold, she had begun attending a Yoga class in order to rebuild her physical strength. With her style no longer cramped by her demanding mother, she had ceased to suffer from cramp in her legs. The main purpose of Anna's visit on this occasion was to discuss the possibility of subtly introducing the use of *Aura-Soma* energies into her mother's life. But that is another story.

Nancy

The name of Bottle No. 55: Clear/Red, the Christ Bottle, refers not to the historical figure of Jesus, but to the energy of the Christ consciousness, which is something to which we all may aspire without blasphemy.

The bottle is about light and inspiration entering the physical world. It is about the energy to work for that to which we are committed; and sacrificial love. It is to do with awakening, and with our strength of purpose: the strength to do that which is necessary and, if necessary, to say no. It can indicate a practical idealist, a spiritual pioneer who is generous and committed. It may, conversely, show that the person is in a state of anger and deep grief.

Nancy came to attend a Foundation Course. She was a young woman of very striking beauty, in the fullest bloom of her mid-twenties. There hung over her, through her lovely smile, an air of deep sadness. The first impression she gave was of a grave seriousness of purpose: deeply attentive and thoughtful. She was the first student that week to book a private consultation. She was very firm and clear in the bottles she chose, losing not a second of time in her quiet determination to hear what the bottles might have to tell her. In second place was Clear/Red.

In *Aura-Soma* the second bottle addresses most specifically the issues with which the person is ready to deal at that point in their life. The remainder of the selection is vitally necessary as well: it enables us to build up a picture of the individual and the situation presented.

Nancy's recent story was one of shattering loss. A year ago she had met the love of her life. After a few months she had become engaged to him and they had planned to marry shortly afterwards. Six weeks later the young man was involved in a car crash and died immediately. Her pain, seven or so months on, was still deep: she was suffering the loss of the soulmate, the person whom she felt to be the missing half of herself.

Nancy was someone with a great love for humanity and a desire to do something which would benefit her fellow men. She wanted to integrate the experience and to reach out to those in pain; but she knew that until she could begin to heal her own deep wound there was little that she could do for anyone else.

She was working in the buying department of a large company. Previously quite keen about the job, she now acted merely from duty, waiting out the hours each day until she could go home and be alone. She had noticed, ironically, that it was only in being alone that she could escape from the overwhelming sense of loneliness which she felt around other people. She rarely, however, cried.

Nancy was trying to make sense of the experience; and she was attempting to find the strength to cope with the grief and come out the other end. In such cases there are no easy answers. A meeting with *Balance* can help to create a space in which a person can look at their life path on a soul level: the unconscious choices they make; the situations, however painful, which they attract and which may ultimately promote their growth. Here was someone who had unconsciously chosen a path of self-sacrifice and who had the potential to bring the light of understanding into that suffering. She saw that she must let the tears be shed before the energy could flow again. She saw the passionate anger which she had never expressed at such a bitter blow of fate. If that were not communicated it must needs turn inwards and fester. She saw, too, her potential for energy and passion and commitment.

Nancy came for consultations every few months for the next year or so after that first occasion. The experience of the Foundation Course gave powerful momentum to the process of her healing, which continued with the twice-daily use of the Clear/Red bottle for the first month. She used it around the lower abdomen and on the crown of the head, in line with the energy centres indicated by the colours in the bottle. She reported that the first month showed significant changes: gradually she began to move outside herself, reconnecting with her old friends and colleagues.

The process is continuing; and Nancy is someone who has completed the *Aura-Soma* training courses, having come initially only in the hope of finding a little light for herself. She now works in a small way with the bottles in her spare time; she finds this work increasingly enthralling.

PINK

The chakra picture shows Pink existing within the Red: neither above it nor below, but within the upper part of its sphere. It is an aspect of the Red energy. If we wish to make a Pink paint, we simply take White paint and mix in a small quantity of Red. Similarly the Pink energy is the Red with the White light shone through it. It is helpful to ponder a little on the Pink as an aspect of the Red, as an understanding of the quality of Pink gives us an opportunity to grasp something of the meaning of the paler colours in general.

Pale colours have in the past been looked upon as diluted energy. In *Aura-Soma* the pale colours are viewed from another perspective: they are seen as clarifications of the true light and the true vibrational energy of the hue which they represent. These paler colours are colours which let through the light, the truth of their brilliance. They are closer in nature to the pure White light and therefore of a higher vibrational energy than the deeper hues.

This does not mean, however, that the choice of a paler colour in any way indicates a superiority in the person who has chosen it. It is easy to become involved with and excited about one or another colour (hue or shade or tint), but each colour is merely a reflection of what is: where the person is in their particular journey; what are the current concerns, preoccupations, difficulties, strengths and joys. The pale colours are seen as more intense than their darker relations. This may indicate that a person choosing them is drawn to the higher spiritual aspects of their own personality and is willing to let through the White light into the colours which clarify these aspects, and their situation in life. Thus this person may in some senses see more clearly. By contrast, the choice of tints may also suggest that there has been a great deal of affliction and hardship of one sort or another: the very process of such clarification inevitably involves purification, with its consequent suffering. Such a person, therefore, may well have some difficulty in reconciling themselves to existence on the physical plane. This may be someone who, for one reason or another, is unwilling to 'get down to earth'.

Pink contains the energy of Red. It is also a separate colour of its own. Unlike Pale Blue, for instance, or Pale Green, this colour is not known as Pale Red, but as Pink, a colour with its own name and its own personality. Perhaps this is part of what accounts for the special quality of the Pink energy: it is frail, yet, like porcelain, this frailty contains great strength.

The cherry blossom appears in the spring, a flower of translucent, almost ethereal beauty, symbolizing new life with all its wonder, purity and frailty. On each tree it lasts a mere seven days, reminding us that physical life is temporal; its very mortality is part of its beauty. The beauty is in the moment. Here is a reminder to accept and receive the life force in each moment and breath of our physical life.

Another unique quality of the Pink is given by the fact that it brings together the two ends of the rainbow, or the chakra system: the White light at the very top, above and beyond the rest, and the Red light at the base. It is, literally, the bringing of the light into the Red area.

There is duality in everything: Red sometimes represents the masculine energy, but it stands also for the feminine, mothering energy of the earth. Pink is a balance colour of the masculine and feminine forces, the masculine being seen as the White light, the active creative light of pure spirit, and the feminine as the deep Red. The Red is the mother earth, our root centre, the world upon which we walk. The White light is the crown, the father, or God. When these two combine in people, in a balanced state of union between masculine and feminine forces, Pink is created. It is an energy of harmony and love that joins man and woman together in balanced light.

Thus, both in man and woman, Pink is associated with the capacity for reproduction, for the giving of the self to create new life: the womb is a powerful symbol of that which is willing to extend itself to make space for another. The nurturing quality of the Pink also offers us the possibility of finding an inner balance and harmony between the masculine and feminine energies within ourselves so that we may become complete. Before the outer balance between men and women can be truly realized, the male must embrace the feminine within himself, and the female must acknowledge and empower that aspect of herself which is masculine. Pink is the total acceptance of ourselves and others which is unconditional love: it is the love which allows things to be, exactly as they are. Within this nurturing ground of the Pink, both masculine and feminine may blossom and thrive.

Love is the movement upwards towards the light; towards self-acceptance and self-knowledge. Fear is the movement downwards towards darkness, the shadow, ignorance. Pink is the antidote for fear. Unconditional love is the ground within which all may accept themselves without judgement, and thus accept others. Compassion begins at home: it begins with our letting go of the need to criticize and judge ourselves; in learning to treat ourselves as we would have others treat us. In loving ourselves, we enable others to do the same. This is not self-indulgence; it is the reverse. Real love can be the most challenging force in our lives. For each of us to learn to love, honour and respect ourselves is a vital challenge if we wish to end violence and conflict and hatred.

Anthony de Mello, in *The Song of the Bird*, tells a story which is a simple but profound illustration of the Pink energy. The story is entitled 'Don't Change':

> I was a neurotic for years. I was anxious and depressed and selfish. Everyone kept telling me to change.
>
> I resented them, and I agreed with them, and I wanted to change, but simply couldn't, no matter how hard I tried.
>
> What hurt the most was that, like the others, my best friend kept insisting that I change. So I felt powerless and trapped.
>
> Then, one day, he said to me, 'Don't change. I love you just as you are.'
>
> Those words were music to my ears: 'Don't change. Don't change. Don't change … I love you as you are.'
>
> I relaxed. I came alive. And suddenly I changed!
>
> Now I know that I couldn't really change until I found someone who would love me whether I changed or not.

The colour of such unconditional acceptance is Pink, and by offering that to ourselves we begin to change the energy which we radiate to others and therefore the response which we receive.

There is a universal, largely unconscious, thirst for Pink: in other words a thirst for that which accepts and loves us exactly as we are, without requiring us to perform, conform or change. The Pink is the colour which most rapidly disappears from the Balance bottles as unconsciously people draw towards themselves that vibration of which they have the greatest need.

Frequently, for example, this may happen during the course of a workshop: some or even many of the bottles will change from Pink to Clear, sometimes within a few hours.

The universal nurturing value of the Pink energy has come to be recognized in some unexpected places. In prisons, for example, it is used to paint the walls which house violent criminals, as it has been found to pacify them if used for a short time. Horticulturalists have begun to use Pink light on a large scale to promote the health and growth of roses, which flourish under the influence of this vibration.

Where Red is passion, Pink is compassion. As the love develops and turns from passion towards compassion and tenderness, the roses may be Pink rather than Red. Where the love in the Red may sometimes be conditional, a passion which seeks possession and satisfaction, the love in the Pink is of a different quality: it is a love without terms or conditions. It is the love which gives without counting the cost, and without expectation of reward. This may also be an attribute of the Red: the Christ energy demonstrates the absolute nature of the love which is prepared to make the ultimate sacrifice. The Pink love is qualitatively different: it is quieter. It is the love of a parent for the child, or the gardener for his plants. It is empathy, tenderness and intuition.

Intuition is inner teaching, the inner voice. In providing the ground upon which we may find self-acceptance, Pink helps us both to hear others and to be heard. There is thus a connection between the Pink energy and the function of hearing. It helps to connect us with the voices of others, and with the sound at our own centre, the still small voice within.

Pink is the colour of childhood: of dreams, of fantasies. Think of a Pink elephant: it is the symbol of unreality. The Rose-coloured spectacles are what we wear when we perceive life as we should like it to be rather than as it actually is. Pink may sometimes be that aspect of our personalities which, Peter

Pan-like, never grows. In this aspect Pink is healing; it gives us a link to greater understanding gained through innocence and purity. It is the colour of the inner child; it helps us to come to terms with the child hidden within, giving it help and warmth and space. Every one of us has a child hiding somewhere within our own breast: it is the aspect which remains open, susceptible and sensitive. It is also the part of ourselves which needs to be cherished and healed before we can blossom and find our full potential.

A consequence of the childlike attributes of the Pink energy is its ability to rejuvenate us. I had worked with *Aura-Soma* for a while, and knew, in theory, of the usefulness of 'thinking Pink' in order to regain youthfulness, when I had to renew my passport. I was astonished to notice that the new passport photograph showed someone who looked considerably younger than the person who had been photographed ten years previously. I refrain from sharing the evidence within these pages on the grounds that if any of us looks like our passport photograph then, Pink or no Pink, we are not fit to travel ...

Within the warmth and the tenderness of the Pink there is, of course, great vulnerability. Frequently the selection of a lot of Pink indicates a need for Pink: someone in great need of love and acceptance. Candy floss is sweet and Pink and mostly made of air: it symbolizes the pretty, feminine, sweet exterior which craves attention and love but which feels insubstantial. Like a candle in the wind, this person's hold on life may be very frail. It may be very hard for such a person to be grounded and to find their own strength. Such a person may have experienced great difficulty, in their early years, in finding love in any form at all. At whatever subconscious level, they may have felt their very survival to be threatened by the lack of nurturing.

A man who is heavily drawn towards the Pink may have

difficulty in getting into touch with his own masculinity. This may perhaps be the consequence of 'smother love' in his childhood.

Pink indicates a sensitive soul, both in the emotional sense and in a spiritual one. It may indicate someone who is very open to the fire vibrations, to the communication of spirit: a sensitive or a natural medium, one who is open to other dimensions.

What about the journey? What about Pink as the en-light-ened form of the Red? Pink is Red with the light shone through. There is therefore a dual possibility: Pink may indicate the overcoming of the major difficulties in the Red, or the reverse. It may show that the unresolved Red issues are particularly intense. This, of course, depends upon the person who has chosen the colours. Only a live selection will give the true picture in any individual case.

The Red issue of survival is all-pervading: the first, most fundamental, issue of the human condition. It appears first and foremost as a physical concern, and repercusses on the physical and on the emotional level for much of a person's life. Anxiety around this difficulty thus absorbs a considerable proportion of our energy. What if we shine the light into this issue? Maybe we shall find that it is even more pressing a concern than we had realized, or maybe we can learn to modify and redirect the energy we expend. Once we detach ourselves a little from the disquietude that this question has caused, the energy can be transmuted and transformed. The anger and the frustration of the Red can become the en-light-ened nurturing of the Pink. We can discover what our real needs are and nurture those, building ourselves up rather than destroying ourselves by anticipation and over-concern for food and warmth and shelter. Thus the possibility is for new beginnings, the awakening to the new self.

Red carries the tendency towards reactiveness, towards

allowing events and people to control the way that we behave. If we shine the light into this tendency, again creating Pink, we can find a little detachment. Thus in the Pink we can step back and retain our power to behave as we consider appropriate in every situation. Instead of 'seeing Red', we can loosen the threads, softening the various knots of anger and resentment and frustration, and find ourselves 'in the Pink'.

With our arrival on earth, we first experienced separation from the source: from the mother, and from something far more distant and primeval, the very source of creation. To overcome the initial fear around survival is thus to pave the way towards a later stage of the adventure, the true discovery of our individuality. In choosing not to react automatically to every challenge and difficulty, but rather to respond, we choose to become creative and to channel the power of our individual choice.

Anger may thus plant a seed which, through the light of awareness, leads to our awakening: it may be transmuted to passion, commitment, tenderness and creativity; resentment to acceptance; frustration to inventiveness.

Pink is the colour of comfort, the colour of love: a colour which eases troubled hearts, which soothes away all hate, all pain. As the Red blood is essential to the life of the body, so Pink is essential to the life of the heart and the soul.

CORAL

As the journey progresses, we move upwards a little from the Red area; before we reach the next major energy centre, the Orange, we come into the region of the Coral.

At the moment of birth, we felt our separation from the Source, and yet remained absolutely dependent physically upon another person: chiefly, and most usually, the mother. Gradually, as we found our feet, there dawned a new state of awareness: we became conscious of ourselves as part of a group. The dependency was still absolute: even Tarzan in the jungle required the protection and nurturing of Great Apes acting as proxy parents. Yet there were subtle alterations. Our needs became more complex than in our first infancy when by and large we were satisfied provided the milk arrived regularly and we were kept warm and clean. Such simplicity was not to last long: somehow a consciousness dawned in us of our need for love and acceptance; little by little, we became aware of our vulnerability.

Coral is a subtle and powerful energy, and one which has only come to conscious awareness quite recently in all but a few cultures. Shamanic traditions such as the Native American Indians have a better understanding of Coral than we do in our own contemporary culture. Ancient societies such as the Tibetans, and the Mayans and Aztecs, have made use of Coral in their art.

In our own culture it is almost like a new discovery. It did not appear within the *Aura-Soma* range until bottle number 87, about seven or eight years into the process. Some have called it the new Christ ray: the ray which will help us to get into touch with the Christ quality of energy and to ground it through our own individual contribution. It still consists predominantly of the Red energy. The new ingredient within the Red is the Yellow. It is called the love wisdom ray: that ray which combines the love energy of the Red/Pink with the wisdom energy of the Yellow/Gold. In terms of the way in which we assess colour composition, the ratio is two parts Red to one part Yellow.

Coral is the colour which originates from the sea. Some years ago I was taken in a glass-bottomed boat across a Turquoise sea to look at some Coral reefs. It was a glorious and beautiful sight: a great, subtle work of art. The beauty of Coral has long been recognized and used in the making of necklaces.

Let us consider an image. Look at the ocean, or think of it. See where the sea touches the shore, moving gently over it, the surface of the body of the earth. This is an act of love. The sea is representative of our great lover: she flows in continual rhythm and cycle with her other selves, the moon and the earth. She is the provider of all, providing us with sustenance, with water in order to survive, in order to cleanse. And yet in her body she contains life of her own unique nature: the fish, the whale, the dolphin, the squid. All these animals exist within her body, which is used to sustain them and to sustain us. The Coral is the boundary; it is a protective layer which is formed through the lovemaking of the sea and the land. As the sea greets her husband, the father, the physical land, the product of this lovemaking is a barrier, a new energy, devoid of each, containing both. Think of the Great Barrier Reef, the greatest coral structure in the world: it forms a natural breakwater off the whole Eastern coast of Queensland in Australia for hundreds of miles. The water between a reef and the shore is a lagoon, and it is protected by the reef from large ocean waves. Such a lagoon gives shelter to shellfish and many other small and vulnerable creatures.

So the Coral is very protective. It shelters others; yet, being very vulnerable, it also has great need for protection for itself. Building on the home of its ancestors, it is absolutely unable to exist alone: its life depends upon being part of a close-knit structure. It cannot travel to obtain its food, and is thus dependent upon food being carried towards it by the sea: it feeds by ingesting small animals and plants drifted by the water within reach of its tentacles.

The Coral reef itself is highly sensitive and susceptible to damage from many sources. Ecologists monitor the condition of the reefs in order to measure the levels of pollution in the ocean, since it is the Coral which dies first whenever harmful substances are present. Coral beds are dying because of the way in which mankind is behaving towards the earth. Residing under the water, the Coral acts as a reminder to us to look at our own subconscious motives which, if they are killing the Coral, must ultimately, too, kill us.

Yet this is not the limit of the sensitivity of Coral: it is not only polluting substances in the water to which the Coral is vulnerable. It cannot stand temperatures below about 68°F and must therefore live close to the Equator. Nor can it tolerate violent waves, which break off parts of itself which then turn to sediment and choke it. Nor can it stand water which is entirely still, since without the gentle currents which transport its food it would starve.

The Coral keeps its shell on the outside; this guards and protects the soft vulnerable fleshy part of itself, which is hidden away deep inside. It provides its own barrier against the violent winds and waves of its own experience, against the heat of passion and the coldness of rejection and starvation. So too the person drawn towards this ray is likely to keep his feelings, and even his nature and his essence, private. Such a person may well have suffered some form of abuse. He will be anxious to avoid displaying much of himself for fear of pain.

Here, then, is an organism which wonderfully symbolizes the human being at a certain stage of our development: before we are ready to attempt to discover our individual nature; when we are soft and infinitely sensitive. It is a ray of deep warmth and tenderness, of generosity and sometimes of a fresh, childlike spontaneity which is purely instinctive. There is the possibility of great empathy within the Coral; existing so close to those around, we feel their joy and pain as our own. Bringing the wisdom ray into the intuition which exists already within the Pink, the Coral enables us to develop that intuition to a fine degree of tuning. Such intuition may be a highly developed spiritual strength.

Coral, by the very physical structure which connects it with its ancestors, has a deep link with the past. The possibility within the Coral is for us to connect with the deep wisdom of the ancient past and to bring it through in a way which is useful for the present time, and for the future.

Part of the experience of being a part of such an intimate and mutually dependent group is the willingness to sacrifice oneself for the good of the whole: for Coral, the very purpose of its existence is to contribute to, and form a part of the group. The other side of this, however, is the dependency which the Coral displays. Physically the Coral organism is parasitic, feeding off other things and unable to look after itself. This is reflected, from time to time, in our emotional life. The choice of Coral may often point to the difficulty which someone experiences in finding the core of their own strength: the adolescent who falls in love with the teacher, or the patient who becomes obsessively dependent upon the doctor are examples of the type of dependency which is characteristic of the Coral. This is someone who, perhaps, has not found a sense of their own worth, and so they may form a pattern in their lives wherein they repeat a chain of dependency, attracting one situation after another in which the love which they feel for another cannot be returned. Hence, for example, a young woman who repeatedly falls in love with men who are already committed to someone or something else: priests, for instance, or married men.

Coral may thus signify that there are relationships which need to be resolved before the person may proceed to the next stage of the journey. They may need help in overcoming deception inflicted on them by others or by themselves. Capable of deep compassion, the person drawn towards Coral may need to discover compassion for themselves. The choice of Coral may indicate that the person is ready to deal with some intense issues which have caused them deep pain in the past: the wisdom and the caring in the Coral create an atmosphere in which it feels safe at last to re-examine these painful situations which have long been kept under lock and key. Similarly, such a person may be ready to look at some intense experience of shock, in this same context of caring and warmth. There are occasions when shock or trauma has been very deeply experienced and where the Orange ray is too direct to contemplate. In such a situation the Coral may provide a gentler energy with which to confront it.

The remedy for so many of these situations is to find the wisdom to love ourselves. Only when we have learned to care for ourselves will our relationships become nurturing ones; only when we honour the value of our own selves and lives as a magnificent gift from the Creator will we truly value others. When we travel on aeroplanes we are given instructions on what to do in an emergency: we are told to put on our own oxygen mask before attempting to put one on a child. This is a useful metaphor for the spiritual and emotional process of loving ourselves. We cannot give what we do not have; therefore if we pay attention, and cherish ourselves, only then will we truly cherish others.

Coral is a ray of great intensity. While the shock and trauma may be deep, and there may be a fear of letting go which is almost literally paralysing, fixing us to the spot like one brick to another, equally deep is Coral's strength. In the Coral state it is possible to achieve heightened states of awareness which are experienced as bliss and ecstasy: a feeling of total joy and participation in the unity of creation.

Coral is a psychical storehouse of power. It can be used to amplify and strengthen our intention, our heart power and our thought power. While at times it can be seen as brittle and in need of assistance to soothe the jagged edges of its nature, it is above all, in its natural state, powerfully protective. It must be looked upon rather as a battery for spiritual energy, power, illumination and knowledge.

Coral can be used to calm the mind that is fighting between the masculine and feminine part of its own nature. It is the compromise; it is the harmonizer; it is the blender of these two energies. It brings thought into feeling, and reason into intuition. Coral is a blanket; a battery; a focus. It is a concentration of energy. It is a colour of balance, a colour of peace, a colour of harmony; and a colour of energy and strength. It is a mixture of rhythm, harmony, and nature.

Eleanor

Let us look at an example of the Coral energy in action: Eleanor looked for all the world like the young woman who had everything. She was beautiful, and wealthy; she was married to an eminent and popular man, and they lived in style in a large and glamorous house where Eleanor divided her time between her two children and the whirl of an ever-full social calendar.

There are only, at present, three *Balance* bottles containing Coral: Eleanor chose all three of them, in the first and second and third positions. The consultation revealed that the reality of her life was that Eleanor felt isolated by her position and her wealth. She had a deep loyalty to her husband: while he had generally in the past treated her with mild affection, they spent almost no time together except in the company of their many acquaintances, most of whom were connected with his work. When they were not either entertaining at home or out at a function, Eleanor was alone with the children. She had recently begun drinking in the evenings after the children had gone to bed; and the drunken state in which her husband had found her on his return had produced some heavy scenes.

Eleanor had grown up within a similar situation to that which she was creating now, often wishing as a child that her parents would separate as the only way she saw of their ending the fights. Neither parent had been emotionally available to meet her needs, but had lavished her first with toys and later with expensive clothes.

All the Coral issues were here: dependency and the deep need to feel herself as part of a close-knit group, unrequited love, deep fears and doubts around her sense of self-worth, the deeply vulnerable core hidden within a very beautiful shell. There were also the Coral gifts: the care with which she nurtured and protected her children, the sensitivity, the sense of beauty, the warmth and tenderness of Eleanor's nature.

All this was discussed, and Eleanor applied the Coral through *Balance* for several weeks before returning to say that she had decided she would like to attend a Foundation Course. This was actually to be the first thing she would have done independently and outside the home since her marriage 10 years previously.

Gradually over the next six months Eleanor's bouts of drinking lessened, and so did the conflicts with her husband. She found a part-time job with an interior design company, apprenticing herself to one of the partners in the hope of developing a practical use for one of her natural skills.

ORANGE

Orange is the colour of the sacral chakra, the second major energy centre of the body. It is composed of Red and Yellow in equal parts. It combines the physical, earthly energy and vitality of the Red with the energy of the Yellow which is the prana, or chi, the energy made available to us by the universe, part of which we take in via the solar plexus.

Orange is a colour of enormous vitality and strength. Oranges are well-known as a source of health and vitality; and they grow only in countries near to the Equator or in the Southern Hemisphere where the sun shines long and hot. Near to the lower end of the spectrum, it is also a colour of great warmth: it brings to mind the heat of the sun, and the fireside warmth of glowing embers.

Here is an example of the powerful physical effect of colour: a London factory had a bright and cheerful canteen whose walls were painted Blue. It was kept at a steady temperature of 21°C, but the workers complained repeatedly that they felt cold. When the temperature was raised by several degrees they continued to feel cold and to wear extra clothing when sitting in that room. After a time the Blue of the walls was replaced by Orange, at which point the workers found that the higher temperature was too hot! The temperature was returned to 21°C and everyone was happy, and warm.

The Orange area is the deepest part of the intestine, through which we absorb the energy from our food, and also assimilate experience. It relates to the colon, the bladder and the gall bladder, which all play a vital part in the digestion of energy and the elimination of waste. It is the area of our gut feelings and gut wisdom. In Buddhist philosophy it is the hara, the seat of the being through which we may connect with the deepest stillness, wisdom and bliss.

Orange represents the region through which the life force begins to leave the body in deep shock or near-death; and it is also the area which houses the spleen, part of whose function is to make energy from the subtle realms available to the physical body.

The Orange energy is thus powerfully physical and powerfully spiritual. It is an oxygenator: it increases the supply of the life force available to us on the directly physical level and the subtle levels, helping us to convert prana, or chi, into energy which can be used by the physical body. The converse is also true: Orange is the physical strength and the gathering of physical energy to sustain the subtle bodies which vibrate on a lower level, in other words those subtle bodies most immediately surrounding the physical. Orange is balance, equilibrium, strength, sustenance, and physical growth. It is the building block of development. It is stimulation of the senses, accentuation of the feelings of the body. Orange also implies power and mastery over the physical universe. This manifests in a number of ways. Orange represents the stage in our journey when, as toddlers, we learn to walk, to explore our immediate universe, and to begin to express our experience. It can also be associated with a state of evolution in which someone may renounce the material and choose the meditative way. Orange contains the possibility for fiery transformation on several levels. It also carries the most unexpected possibility: a relationship with machinery which renders it a most useful resource when the car or the computer refuses to start (*see* Pomanders, page 127).

Orange is the expression of optimism and joy, of a strong vital force. In the factory quoted above, equipment which had originally been Grey was re-painted to Orange. This was found to motivate the workforce. Also, not only was the incidence of work-related accidents reduced, but the labourers began to sing as they worked!

Orange represents the stage in the journey when we begin to develop an awareness of ourselves as separate from the mother, the father, and the group; and yet, still dependent, we have to grow and find our strength before we can exist outside that group. It can thus be associated with the positive nurturing of ourselves which leads to our spiritual and emotional development, as well as the physical. In contrast, if our needs for nurturing are not met and the strength is not found, Orange may indicate an extreme lack of self-esteem. Sometimes it points to a deep indecisiveness which comes from fear. 'Which way shall I go?'

Orange has a great intensity and power: it is very stimulating and there are few people who would choose to wear it in quantity or for any length of time. It indicates someone of a gregarious, sociable nature: a person who enjoys being part of a group rather than one who enjoys her own company. The person drawn to Orange is willing to be seen. In good emotional health, this person functions well in a group and her outgoing nature will bring groups together and cause things to happen.

The opposite extreme may on occasion present itself as a challenge. Orange may indicate total disassociation and fragmentation, where everything falls apart. It may indicate a shock so extreme that the person feels shattered. Or, on a wider scale, it may accompany a time when the old order of things collapses and anarchy appears to reign. Orange is the colour which indicates such fragmentation and collapse, but it is also the energy which heals it. It re-aligns and re-establishes things in their appropriate place.

As we move into this stage of the journey, our survival needs become more subtle and more complicated. The cement-like structure which reassured us in the early months and years is loosening. This represents the possibility of freedom, but it also brings up our deepest and most irrational fears. We are entering the web of relationship, where in order to ensure that our survival needs are met we feel the need to please those upon whom we depend. We begin to seek approval, or sometimes to rebel. In imbalance, Orange may indicate someone who has learned to manipulate others in the hope of finding security. As with the Coral, the threads which comprise the web of relationships are, in part, threads of fear. What if? How would I survive alone? The Orange and the Coral are the balance colours between the Red/Pink and the Yellow energies. By loosening and dissolving the threads of fear we make space for something new to flourish: the unconditional love, which recognizes and respects oneself and others. This is the stuff of the eternal web: the web of love, which supports and cultivates our mutual growth.

Relationship is therefore one of the chief issues within the Orange. How we progress through the issues in this chakra, how we balance our connection with those around us with our developing separateness sets a pattern for life. Until we have reconciled these two opposing needs we are likely to remain dependent upon others. Here is the foundation for dependency and co-dependency within relationships, the dependent one sitting in the wheelchair, metaphorically speaking, and the co-dependent other pushing it. In dependency we feel unable to cope with life's challenges and will turn to another; in co-dependency our sense of value hangs upon the assurance of being needed. Orange, therefore, is often indicative of addiction, which may take many forms: we may be addicted to a person, a situation, cigarettes, alcohol, or a type of food, to name a few examples. Addictions are those things which we crave and yet which imprison us rather than encourage our freedom and growth.

An obvious context within which dependency issues may manifest is that of sexual relationships. In imbalance, of course, a sexual relationship may be addictive. But within the Orange, also, there is contained joy and bliss. The Orange area relates directly to sexual function, as does the Red; but the Orange speaks more of sex as a joyful form of communication than as a reproductive function. In health, the Orange is not so much a passionate energy as a joyous one.

A negative form of the Orange energy is manifested in cases of sexual abuse, or rape. A preference for Orange, particularly where it appears near the beginning of a selection, frequently indicates that there has been abuse. Sometimes it is the use of the Orange energy which allows a person to release memory blocks around such experiences.

Orange is a shocking colour. It can dazzle and stimulate; it may irritate, but it cannot be ignored. It is the colour of shock. Everything about it is intense. The insights we obtain in the Orange are found through the deepest gut wisdom; where there is humour it is likely to be hysteria; where there is joy it is ecstasy and bliss; where there is fear it is way beyond reason.

Orange is invaluable where the shock and trauma have gone deep: in cases of miscarriage and surgical operations and accidents; after suicide attempts or other close encounters with death. Such shock or trauma may sometimes be associated with experiences in previous incarnations. This can manifest as very deep-seated grief which has been long repressed.

What happens in deep shock? How are we most likely to

react? Will we go with the flow of the experience, calmly and serenely bending and dancing to its rhythm or its beat? It is much more likely that, stunned, we shall stop in our tracks, as though someone had pressed the 'pause' button on some invisible controller. The tendency in shock, at all levels of the being, is to hold on, to go into a kind of paralysis. It is the Orange energy which helps us to assimilate the experience, and ultimately to let go of it. The organs in the Orange region assimilate, but they also eliminate. Imbalance occurs when we hold on: to fear, to shock, or to physical substances which poison the system.

Orange has not often appeared on the scene of fashion. It was a popular colour, however, in the 1960s. For the older generation, this was a time of deep shock. All the old values were turned upside-down; the established order crumbled. For the young this was an energy explosion and a time of joy and optimism unlimited. The vitality was worldwide: in the East and the West, the young found for themselves a new power and an apparent independence. The world burst into song, sexual expression exploded, and addiction became rampant. The independence may only have been skin deep; yet it was nevertheless a time of fiery, powerful change. Orange, incidentally, reappeared in the fashion shops during 1996, and is still much in evidence: only history will tell what its re-emergence may signify. A new vitality? The anticipation of shock? A recovery of optimism and joy? It is clearly an important energy for the time we are in. Maybe it is linked to the gathering of energy for the transition into the next millenium?

While Orange can be an energy which is dynamically and powerfully linked to physical experience, it can also indicate the very opposite. It is the colour of autumn, when the leaves are dying, renouncing their own life to make compost for the new season's growth. It is dying cells which produce the hormone which allows the new plant to take root: what the gardener knows as rooting powder. This is a symbol for a law which governs our spiritual growth: Orange is a reminder that we must die to a part of ourselves in order to create a space for something new. The new leaves must have space to flourish. Orange is the colour of renunciation: a letting go of the physical world in order to experience another dimension. It is the colour of sunsets, of endings which make way for new beginnings. For the seeker, a sunset is a symbol of aspiration: it lifts us beyond the material and the physical. The Buddhist monks wear saffron robes, as a symbol of their willingness to renounce the material world. Here is an example of the dedication which leads to fulfilment and bliss.

Orange may be obsessive, but it carries within it the energy for persistence and dedication. It is the fires of sexuality, sensuality and desire; and it is also the fuel for creative aspiration and renunciation of worldly pleasure. Orange has to do with the prison of dependency and co-dependency; but the gift when such a state is overcome is of bliss and rapture and the deepest possible joy. It is essential food for the body and the soul.

Alan

Bottle No. 26: Orange/Orange, the Shock Bottle/Humpty Dumpty, is for treating the effects of shock and trauma on all levels. If it appears at the beginning of a selection, it almost always means that the person using it has experienced some kind of shock or abuse which needs to be dealt with as the effects of this experience will tend to obscure the rest of the picture.

Alan came initially for a private consultation. He expressed interest in attending a workshop which was scheduled for a week later, and for the intervening week he came and went, alternately asking whether he might join and then finding excuses why it would be impossible.

On this first occasion Alan chose Orange/Orange in first place, and in second place Blue/Orange. The immediate impression which the selection gave was one of shock. Deep shock and trauma; and some kind of abuse. In shock we tend to go into a kind of spasm; a temporary paralysis. The Orange, proclaiming itself loud and clear at the beginning of the selection, indicated that other issues were for the moment overshadowed by an experience which had wounded Alan deeply enough to fix him in a position from which, despite the severe pain it caused him, he was unable to move.

The other bottles in the selection confirmed the strong impression that Alan had, besides the shock, been in the grip of a dependent/co-dependent structure of relationship. This also manifested as addictive patterns of behaviour. It was as though there were threads of fear linking him to those around which had become set like concrete, binding him to a structure which offered little opportunity for growth.

These were the issues generally discussed in the first session. Alan was aware that much of his memory of childhood was blocked. He had for some years been in psychotherapy which had already gone some way to helping him to gain insights into childhood experiences, but try as he would he had been unable to discover what had happened in his childhood which had caused pain acute enough to blank out the memory of it.

Alan began working with the Orange over Orange bottle, the only bottle which needs to be used in a specific way: all around the abdomen and down the left side of the body from the ear lobe to the ankle.

Alan's wife Monica also came for a private consultation. Her issues were a little less dramatic but nonetheless there was clearly a similarity to Alan's pattern of experience.

Eventually, after a great deal of prevarication, Alan courageously took the decision to attend the workshop. It was during the course of that week that he went into crisis.

Halfway through the seminar he decided that he would be unable to attend the remainder of the course: 'something had come up' which was very important so he would not have time to finish the week with us. It was clear that he was facing some very painful issues, and that he was looking for a way out. At that moment he did not believe he would find the courage to go through the process of looking at the stark reality of his earlier experiences. It was vital, however, that he stayed the course rather than going off alone in such an acutely vulnerable state. After some talking he was persuaded to stay.

For most of the next day Alan sat in a corner weeping on his own, before he felt able to talk about the memories which were at last surfacing. These were recollections of abuse beyond many people's imagining: a web, within the family, of incest, rape and attempted murder, which had left Alan confused and terrified throughout his life about relationships, about trust, about the expression of love. Here was a man with humour, sensitivity, and a deep love of children who had dared not trust himself to have children of his own for fear of what he might inflict on them.

His feeling of unworthiness and inadequacy had held him back from a close relationship with his wife, who in her turn had felt rejected and excluded from his life. This situation was temporarily exacerbated by his recollections concerning the behaviour of his family, since he felt soiled and shamed by his association with them. There was some work to be done before he would find the courage to tell his wife the truth about his childhood.

Little by little Alan began to realize that the shame was not his own, and he was able to let go of it and to accept the love of his wife who for years had longed to reach out and support him. As the communication between them increased, they began to entertain the possibility of having children. Alan's psychotherapist told him that in the space of the initial few weeks spent in working intensively with *Aura-Soma* he had made the equivalent of about two and a half years of progress.

GOLD

We are moving, now, away from the base and towards the centre. Gold contains one part Red to two parts Yellow. So something of the Red energy remains: the passion, the courage, and the commitment, for example; and from time to time, perhaps, the resentment and frustration. But the Gold is about something new: it is the move away from dependency and towards finding the individual self.

Words themselves frequently offer us valuable insights. Think about the word God, for example: G-O-D. Add an L and we have the word Gold. Seen within this context, the L stands for the light within the Godhead: the light which pours from the source, though our awareness of it may be deeply buried. Gold is the colour of hidden knowledge and wisdom. As it is rich on the earth plane, it is rich in spirit. It is tempered wisdom, tempered knowledge, tempered enlightenment. Gold is a lifetime's collection of experience and value: the wisdom of the sage. It is the inner knowing which is accumulated through experience. It is profound understanding: the deep wisdom of the past brought through into the present.

Gold is the symbol of riches on all levels. It is the material wealth of precious metal, adorning the rich and powerful, and conferring status and might on those who have it in their possession.

It was long the metal of international currency: the Gold standard represented stability in the world money market. Thus it stood widely in force before the First World War as a mark not only of wealth but of steadiness and security, and for some time after the Second World War it still remained as a method of international payment which served to stabilize exchange rates. Thus it is a sign of constancy, just as the Gold ring of marriage stands for consistency and commitment. It holds things together. The 'Golden Age' evokes a glowing and glorious time: health, wealth and prosperity reigned, and this happy and peaceful state of affairs was guarded and maintained by a strong king at the centre. Such an age is characterized by a feeling of safety and a lack of strife.

Gold has been seen not only as a sign of peace, security and prosperity, but of power and strength: Golden lions protected the ancient temples, and palaces are guarded by Golden gates.

Gold is the metal of royalty: of crowns and jewels. It is prized for its purity and beauty as well as its material worth. It is associated with the royal qualities of judgement, justice and balance, as demonstrated by the wisdom of Solomon.

From Gold stars awarded in Kindergarten school to the crowns of kings and queens, Gold is given as a mark of status and high endeavour. The colour of kingliness, it is awarded as a symbol of initiation, of reaching a high standard of achievement or a position of authority. It is associated with material power and also with spiritual power and holiness: cathedrals, cardinals and Popes are decorated and embellished with Gold. The Eastern hemisphere abounds with statues of their great Buddha which are crafted from Gold. Always the Buddha is seen in a meditative posture, radiating peace and fulfilment: 'silence is Golden'.

We talk of 'going for Gold', when we are aiming high,

striving for the best. Such endeavour may require that we seek the power and strength which lies deeply buried within ourselves. We may struggle to acquire that which we most highly value. This has been exemplified by those throughout history who have sought to dig for Gold within the body of the earth. The search for Gold has contributed greatly to geographical knowledge, the promise of riches encouraging settlement in regions thought to be almost uninhabitable, such as Alaska and the Northernmost reaches of Canada; and the deserts of California and Australia. In 'going for Gold', men have found the spirit of adventure, breaking away from the safety of all that is familiar and secure. The rewards promised are material ones, yet in order to achieve their end such adventurers have had to dig deep into their own internal resources to survive in conditions and climates which are very far from friendly.

To dig for and find Gold was to discover a precious metal of great price, and which represents, on many levels, great power. Gold is an excellent conductor of heat and electricity, in other words it has a powerful capacity for transmitting energy; but it is very resistant to chemical reagents and is therefore virtually incorruptible. Here is the spiritual strength for which it stands. Unaffected by oxygen or alkalis, it does not tarnish. It is known, therefore, as a 'noble' metal.

Gold is a colour, therefore, of dignity and might; and great purity, Gold metal being found often in its natural state unalloyed with other metals. Thus it represents, too, the possibility of finding independence. Its purity means that we can fill our teeth with it and suffer no ill effects.

Thus, in every sense, Gold is associated with the idea of value and worth. It represents assets and qualities which are very precious. We refer to people, ideas or things on which we place a particularly high value as 'Gold dust'. Or we describe someone who is generous and pure as having a 'heart of Gold'.

It is only when we gain a sufficient sense of our own value and worth that we can find the courage to break away from the web of dependency and discover our own selfhood.

Thus Gold, in spiritual terms, is valued not so much as an end product but as a process. 'Somewhere over the Rainbow' there lies a pot of pure Gold. But which end of the rainbow? Is it somewhere way up high, far out of reach? Or is the pot of Gold our own deep inner power and strength which is connected with the wisdom within? Gold, hidden deep inside, is the full power of our potential. The alchemists sought to master the hidden powers which determine the forms of matter: in particular they sought to change base metals, which are corruptible and perishable, into Gold, which is incorruptible and permanent. The alchemists were sincere seekers after knowledge and spiritual truth: the mystic reagent known as the 'Philosopher's stone' was believed to have power over death and corruption. Yet the true process of alchemy is one of spiritual seeking and growth: the transmutation of mankind, symbolized by the base metal, through the touchstone, which is love. Alchemy is an inner journey which purifies and refines; it is the transmutation of negativity and the integration of our own true quality.

Gold is thus recognized, beyond the material level, as the wealth of spirit. Art throughout the centuries has given the symbol of divine wisdom to saints and other enlightened beings, portraying them with a halo of Gold above the crown. The auric body of the more evolved beings is symbolized by the Golden Egg. The Three Wise Men offered, as well as frankincense and myrrh, Gold to the infant Jesus: Gold symbolized the potential to rule the world or to liberate it. It was the Magi's gift to Jesus but it is also the devil's temptation.

Hence the warning which is also contained within the Gold. 'All that glitters is not Gold.' The presence of Gold may register a need for discrimination; a need to examine something in greater depth to uncover its essence. Is it true or false? Gold can have to do with trickery and deception, temptation and delusion. It can be the mirage of the material world, and the guile of spiritual glamour and power. While Gold represents the enticement, it is also our safeguard. Gold can be the protection from all things negative. It is a dense vibrational colour. It is heavy, as Gold is heavy. It is a shield, and sometimes a mask. It keeps those wrapped safely in its colour free from all negativity, all harm, all etheric tampering, all meddlesome vibrations.

Like Orange, Gold also contains the potential for great joy and fulfilment. There is a gradation in intensity from Orange through Gold and into the Yellow energy: several of the same issues are addressed within these three areas, varying in depth and degree. So, for example, the quality of gladness is akin in the Yellow to an everyday kind of happiness; in the Orange it can deepen to the most elevated states of ecstasy and rapture: the Gold comes somewhere between the two. It is something deeper than simply happiness: it is a deep joy, without quite the intensity of the Orange. Similarly, within Gold is the quality of instinctive wisdom, as opposed to the more mental faculty of acquired knowledge which is in the Yellow, and the deepest most penetrating insights, the gut knowledge of the Orange.

Gold also contains deep fear. This also is a feature of the Yellow energy, but again the variation is in its intensity. Whereas the Yellow fear is subject to reason, the fears in the Gold are deep and irrational. They are the fears of things that go bump in the night: fear of darkness; fear of loss; fear of being enclosed in tight spaces. They are fears which are based in the emotions and which relate above all to issues of security. Gold can also indicate that there is deep uncertainty and confusion, which may further compound the fear. *Aura-Soma* encourages us to make friends with our fears, to move willingly into the confusion and the fear in order to discover its lesson. Deep confusion, once processed and reassembled, can be the means towards greater clarity in the end.

The move towards the Gold area is the move towards individuality, and to discovering our worth. Such a move is subject to challenges like all the rest. The challenge here is to balance the state of confidence. A lack of confidence may manifest as fear around accepting our power, a difficulty in embodying our individuality; or it might express itself as false humility. Conversely, an over-supply of confidence might lessen our sensitivity to those around us. Here are the dangers of greed, avarice, and self-righteousness. The ego may become inflated and the individual may seek power and dominance over others, at the expense of his own growth.

Gold is the colour of wisdom and warmth, deep insights and profound joy. It is the halo of saints, who have found the inner Gold and allowed it to radiate, sharing it with the world through the crown of the head. It is the colour of sunshine and the galaxy of the heavenly bodies of planets and stars. It is a rich colour and we have great need of it on this plane.

Let us look now at how some of the colours we have looked at so far can come together within a bottle.

Harold

Harold was a man in his forties who came initially as a journalist to observe some teaching sessions and to interview us for a magazine article. In the course of this he became interested in the process for himself and requested a full consultation.

The therapeutic bottle which he chose was No. 40, Red over Gold. Known as the 'I am' Bottle, the gift within it is a lot of energy and commitment in someone who is likely to be very successful in their work. It shows a lively enthusiastic person who has wisdom and understanding to share with the world.

I had been impressed by the very positive energy which Harold had brought to the work he was doing with us, and by the obvious integrity he showed in the way he went about attempting to understand the nature of *Aura-Soma*.

The consultation brought out something of the fuller picture. Here indeed was someone with enthusiasm, passion and humour, as well as a deep sense of responsibility. He harboured, as well, immense frustration, anger and resentment over his home life in which he felt he had no control at all. Long married to his childhood sweetheart who had early branded herself as an invalid, he had done much of the rearing of children alone, taking them on holidays while his wife preferred to go to a health farm, driving them to and from school and so on. Harold and his wife had long since lived apart effectively but under the same roof, sharing very little communication. She became hysterical if ever Harold went out to anywhere but work, and was vigilant in timing all his activities and ensuring that she knew at every minute of his exact whereabouts. She also had a tendency to undermine his achievements. Being intellectually quite able, she perused and criticized the articles he wrote and never lost an opportunity of calling his attention to whatever it was that he had failed to do. His friends had for many years failed to understand why he had remained in this situation, and as people preferred not to interact with his wife he found that increasingly his only friendships were work ones.

So the question for Harold was 'Why?'. Why had he put himself in this situation? Why was he undermined by the relationship? Why, too, were younger journalists often being given the jobs instead of him?

The Gold in the base of this bottle can show deeply hidden fears. While it shows the capacity for profound insights it also indicates confusion. The 'I am' in the person choosing this combination often needs to be heard and to be understood. He may harbour great doubts about his own value. Emulsifying to Orange, it also speaks of some kind of abuse; and also of dependency and co-dependency. Harold had long since recognized the dependency of his wife upon him, but he had not yet seen the degree of his co-dependency: in other words his need to be needed. Having married a person who in many of her difficult aspects closely resembled his own mother, Harold had yet to see that this situation had provided him with a clear role, in which unconsciously he had hoped to receive the love he only expected to receive by fulfilling the other person's expectations. He had been clearly 'needed' to fetch his wife's pills and do her shopping, in other words, metaphorically speaking, to push her wheelchair. The 'wheelchair' had been not only her prop but also his, providing him with an insurance policy against discovering himself to be worthless.

Awakening came quite rapidly for Harold after this first session. He was conscientious in applying the bottle twice each day. While remaining with his wife, he began consciously to take back his power, talking openly to her with courage and simplicity. He assured her that he would continue to support her, but that in order to do so he must make time too for himself.

Over the ensuing months, as Harold began to change, though with some reluctance, so did his wife. The relationship is not close or active, but much of the fear within it has been overcome and Harold's work is consequently thriving again.

YELLOW

Here we come to the third major energy centre of the body, the solar plexus chakra. We have moved right out of the Red and come to the primary colour Yellow, a hue which has a direct simplicity, being composed from a single ray. This is in contrast to most of the other colours, which are secondary or tertiary colours, combining two or more rays (think, for example, of Green, which is a mixture of Yellow and Blue; or Violet, which combines Blue and Red).

Yellow is the ray of sunshine: the solar plexus is the sun centre of the being. It represents the core of our individuality.

Each person may emerge, as the sun appears out of the sky, individual: separate and unique in quality, though ultimately undivided from the rest of creation. To recognize the unique personal quality is to acknowledge the individual part that each has to play in the unfolding adventure. Shakespeare told us that 'All the world's a stage': the trick is to discover our own particular role on that stage.

Yellow is the colour of prana, the universal life force; and the solar plexus has a major role to play in receiving this life energy which gives us vitality and strength. The solar plexus is the 'spaghetti junction' of the nervous system, the junction where so much information comes together. This is information from our myriad experiences communicated through the neural passages. What will we do with this information? Will we accept it and assimilate it, keeping the solar plexus open and relaxed so that the vital force may enter and circulate, and experience may be incorporated into the individual fabric of our being? Or will the solar plexus tighten into a knot of fear, cramping the soul and giving us indigestion?

The solar plexus has also been called the second brain. It is through this area that we assimilate knowledge. Yellow is therefore associated with knowledge and the sharing of it: with teaching and the dissemination of information. It is closely associated with the function of intellect and thought. The person choosing a lot of Yellow may well have a very active mind: they are probably drawn towards intellectual occupations; maybe towards writing, mathematics or teaching. In the healthy state this is a creative energy. Yellow is creativity and understanding. It is practical thought. It is inspiration, and it can be wisdom; though this is the wisdom that is acquired through learning and thought, rather than the deeper intuitive wisdom of the Gold. It can be the feeling of satisfaction which comes from intellectual achievement. Intellectual acuity may be applied in a negative sense, in which case the Yellow might manifest destructively, as cynicism or sarcasm.

Yellow is uplifting, bringing optimism and good cheer. Sunlight raises the spirits, bringing warmth and gladness and humour; and the lack of it depresses not only the spirit but the body, causing deficiencies of Vitamin D and a lowering of the vital force. Seasonal Affective Disorder (SAD) is a medically recognized condition of sadness, a type of depression which is remedied by the rays of the sun. The person who is drawn to Yellow is likely to be a vibrant and optimistic person who has the ability to make others laugh. They can see the funny side of most situations. They are probably also people who are drawn towards countries drenched in hot sunshine; they may have a past-life connection with Mediterranean countries, and with Egypt or South America. Or they may simply be drawn towards Yellow because they feel like a nervous wreck ...

The ancient Egyptians believed that as the sun set each night it descended to the Underworld, travelling through it to be reborn the next morning. Every morning's sunrise is a new beginning. Yellow is a powerful symbol of new life, of birth and rebirth. It is the healing power which gives regeneration. It is the colour of spring flowers, of aconites and primroses and daffodils. It is the colour of egg yolks and chicks. It is the colour of young souls and youthful enthusiasm: full flesh with the vitality of new creation. Yellow is the colour of invention and innovative thought.

The colour Yellow has a close connection to the White light. Its vibration is lower than that of White light, but it is a bright colour, with great power and strength, and it has the capacity to radiate the energy of White light. We perceive the sun as being Yellow; while in reality it emits the full spectrum of White light. Similarly, we perceive the light radiating from a transparent electric bulb as Yellow. A candle flame burns Yellow, a symbol of everlasting life and of our own inner light.

Yellow is also the colour of the harvest: freshness, nourishment and the reaping of rewards. It is the assimilation of physical nourishment and pranic energy; and also of intellectual material. It is energizing and stimulating, particularly on the mental plane. Yellow is the most stimulating colour for the mental body. Parents who are keen to encourage the mental development of their child would do well to paint her bedroom primrose Yellow.

Yellow is the colour of the individual will. It is the enthusiasm to set out and achieve our goals: the knowledge and belief that in putting our will behind our intention, the aim will be achieved. In an exaggerated form this could become self-centredness, selfishness or self-importance.

What might be the other difficulties within the Yellow chakra? Someone who is 'Yellow bellied' is someone who shows cowardice, allowing the fear to hold them back. They may be terrified of acknowledging their separateness, their individuality, suppressing all that they know and believe in order to avoid conflict. Fear is part of our condition: some of our terrors, particularly those within the Yellow, may be packaged and labelled; the deeper ones are better camouflaged and harder to pin down. The fear is the knot in the solar plexus, the twisted gut. On the physical level the fear may make itself felt in a number of ways: as a problem in the stomach, the kidneys, or the pancreas, for example. Many of the vital organs are contained within this region; or within the Gold and the Orange. Or the disquiet may express itself through the nervous system as anxiety. The solar plexus is also closely related to the skin, so that difficulties which have their origin in the Yellow of the nerve junction might appear as skin irritation in another region of the body.

On an emotional level the fear may manifest in another way: someone suffering great fear may have a need to try to control, to dominate and manipulate those around them. The fear which lies in the Yellow may sometimes be overcome by reason and the power of the intellect, unlike the Gold fear which is buried deep in the recesses of our unconscious. Yellow is mental courage, when we feel the fear but get on and do it all the same.

Like Gold, Yellow sometimes carries confusion; and as with Gold, the very confusion is frequently the means by which we eventually find the greatest clarity of mind. The Pale Yellow, which we see when we shine the light into the Gold, may indicate the most intense confusion and fear; but it is also the route towards the deepest self-knowledge.

Part of the upward movement through the energy centres has been the movement away from dependency and towards independence. Our aim is to stand upright in the world, clear in our own integrity and strength. As we shine the light into the issues of the Yellow we have the possibility of letting go of the need to prove. In our state of dependency we looked for approval outside ourselves, to a figure of authority. The discovery of our true individuality releases us from this need. We find the capacity to say 'OK' to ourselves. When we can find the courage to shine the light on the fear and look at ourselves, we gain access to a new wisdom: that which links us with the universal human condition. Perhaps it is not even quite as serious as we thought ... We can listen to the words of the Zen master Bodhidharma:

'Happy is the man who can laugh at himself, for he will never cease to be amused.'

THE TURNING POINT

We have journeyed through the three major energy centres of the body: three of the colours of the rainbow, and the gradations between them. We have looked at some of the major issues connected with each. Here we reach a crossroads: this is an appropriate moment to pause and take stock of where we have come from and where we might be going. It is also a moment where we can look and see what was happening on my own journey, after the experience of 'Rebirth'.

Aura-Soma is a means through which we may apply the energies of light to our well-being throughout the many different levels of our existence. I had witnessed something of this in the workshop described; nevertheless, I understood little of its theory, and accepted less, in the early days when bouts of training were scattered between episodes of the bizarre drama which then comprised my experience. In being catapulted from one event to the next I had to adopt, literally, a hands-on approach. Life itself was to be my most powerful teacher: in its apparent brutality it would provide a series of potent and forceful opportunities for the discovery of energies of whose existence I had never dreamed. Armchairs are alluring, but it is the pins and needles, the shocks and anxieties, which wake us up. The energies of light were applied quite literally to these events to provide understanding as well as remedies.

One of the next things that happened was that I decided to leave home. I had no idea where we would go, the children and I. The capital which I had inherited from my parents many years previously had all been invested in the house: it was therefore wiped out. For years my only significant work had been to look after the children. Nobody pays one for that; and besides we lived miles from anywhere with no possible means of finding the kind of rent which would be payable in a more populated area. Nevertheless, go I must. Fortunately it was now summer, so we were able to camp out in relatives' spare rooms or holiday caravans. Then the autumn term arrived and we squeezed ourselves together in the spare bedroom of a generous friend.

Within a few months Mike and Claudia came to the rescue of all of us, offering us the use of a cottage which they and their family had just vacated. It was warm and cosy. It had a fitted kitchen; walls which were not only plastered but papered and decorated; carpets and curtains and lovely warm radiators. It was a gift sent straight down from Heaven. For three days, enlisting the help of long-suffering friends, I reclaimed from the farmhouse what furniture belonged to us and created within this little cottage the first home we had known for over two years.

The relief, however, of finding a sort of independence and a home we could call our own was shortlived. It was the middle of the third night in that cottage, just as all the furniture had found its place, when my son Stephen woke me, complaining of severe abdominal pain. Within a couple of

Plate 1:
'I have often heard of the response of people when meeting *Aura-Soma* for the first time. Many people are lyrical about it. They talk about rainbows. They talk about coming home.'

Plate 2
Rebirth. The bottles are the focal point of every *Aura-Soma* training course, their colours radiant and joyful, resembling the exotic tones of silks and orchids, precious stones and tropical fish.

Plate 3
Colour Medicine. The working of Balance is multidimensional. Within each bottle we may find the combination of several different natural methods for restoring the balance of the system.

Plate 4
Bottles 45 & 46. The Magenta in Bottle 45 showed Rosemary's blend of passion and tenderness; the Turquoise her need for creative communication through the heart.

Plate 5
Bottles 51 & 52. In the second place, Bottle 52 shows a problem. Pink is most likely to be related to the mother: it could indicate either smothering or neglect.

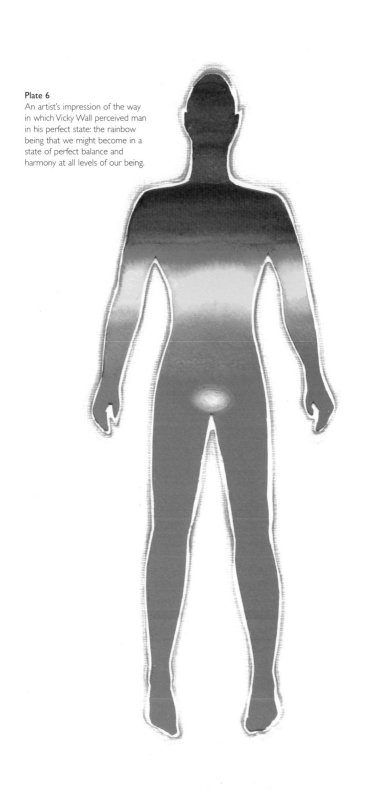

Plate 6
An artist's impression of the way in which Vicky Wall perceived man in his perfect state: the rainbow being that we might become in a state of perfect balance and harmony at all levels of our being.

Plate 7
Bottles 55 & 56. Bottle 55, chosen by Nancy, is the Christ Bottle and is about light and energy entering the physical world.

Plate 8
The Energy Bottle. Red/Red is a re-energizer, helping us to connect with the basic energy and enthusiasm for life and love.

Plates 9 & 10

Within each bottle is held a unique formula of energies from three kingdoms. The first of these is the plant kingdom. A bottle includes, in its top half, aromatic essential oils contained within other plant oils: these are coloured by plant dye of a very high quality. This oily mixture is perfectly balanced and resting upon a base fraction, which contains water of a very high purity with the addition of the watery herbal extracts of plants.

Plate 11

Bottles 25 & 26. Bottle 26, Orange/Orange, called the Shock Bottle or Humpty Dumpty, appeared in first place in Alan's selection. In this place it indicates that the person using it has experienced some kind of shock or abuse that needs to be dealt with.

Plate 12

Bottles 40 & 41. Bottle 40, Red over Gold, is known as the 'I am' Bottle. Chosen by Harold, it shows a lively enthusiastic person who has wisdom and understanding to share with the world.

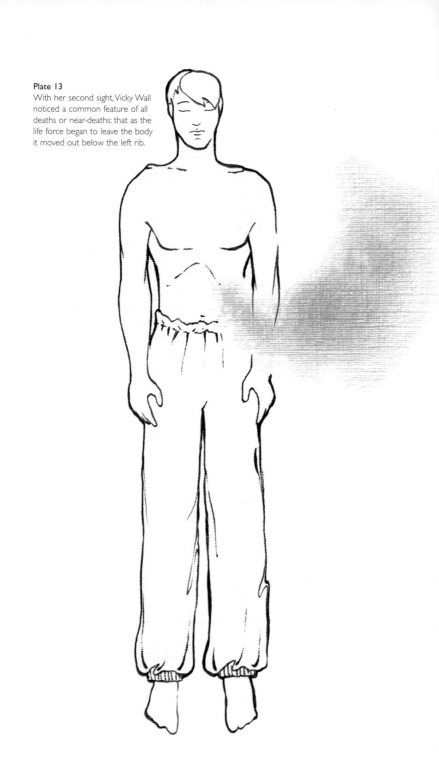

Plate 13
With her second sight, Vicky Wall noticed a common feature of all deaths or near-deaths: that as the life force began to leave the body it moved out below the left rib.

Plates 14 & 15

Pomanders and Quintessences: Pomanders are created from herbs preserved and presented in a base of alcohol. They can be applied by the hands directly on to the aura. Quintessences are similar to but paler than Pomanders; they are also more potent and are the subtlest of all the products in the *Aura-Soma* range.

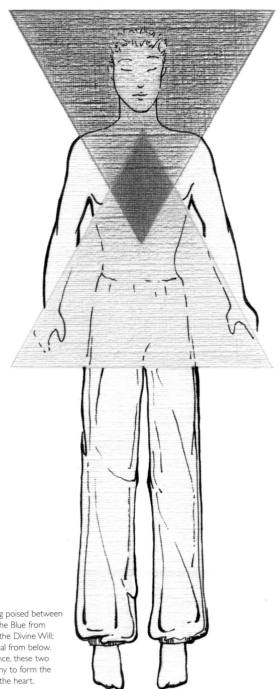

Plate 16
Man can be seen as being poised between two triangles of energy: the Blue from above, which represents the Divine Will; the Yellow of the individual from below. In a state of perfect balance, these two come together in harmony to form the green within the area of the heart.

Plate 17

Bottles 21 & 22. Chosen by
Camilla, Bottle 21 – Green/Pink
– is known as New Beginning
for Love and is a bottle that,
when indicated as a gift, shows
a strong mature person.

Plate 18

Bottles 43 & 44. Bottle 43 –
Turquoise/Turquoise – is the bottle of
Creativity. Its strength is the ability to
communicate creatively, and widely, from
the heart; the communication is often
through art or music or dance. In Paul's
selection, part of the challenge it showed
was his unwillingness to connect with
the deeper aspects of himself.

Plate 19
Bottles 1, 2, 3. Bottle 3 – Blue/Green – is known
as the Heart Bottle. It relates above all to the
heart and the emotional aspect of life.

Plate 20
Bottles 15, 16, 17. Bottle 16 is called the Violet Robe. It indicates someone who has a strong connection with their spiritual aspect, and is chosen by those involved in helping others in the transformative process. It comforted Roy's father, Fred, as he approached death.

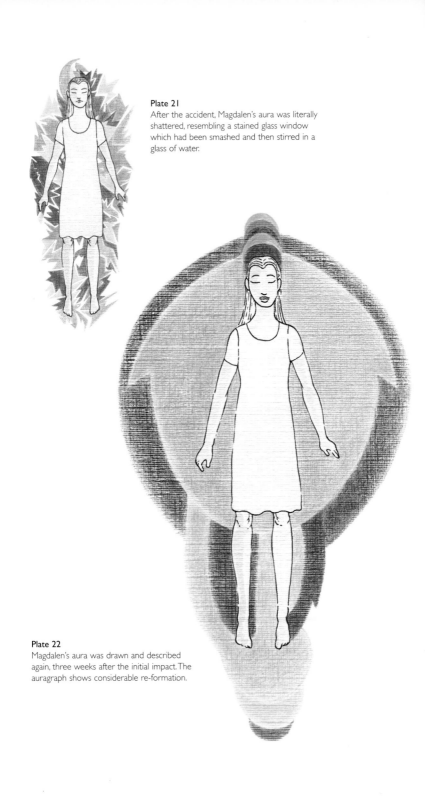

Plate 21
After the accident, Magdalen's aura was literally shattered, resembling a stained glass window which had been smashed and then stirred in a glass of water.

Plate 22
Magdalen's aura was drawn and described again, three weeks after the initial impact. The auragraph shows considerable re-formation.

Plate 23
Two months later another auric
picture was drawn. This shows that
the rainbow-like formation which
had begun to show above
Magdalen's head had by this time
extended its reach down her body.

Plate 24
We gain much insight into the nature of the Clear light from its name. The name implies clarity: the phrase 'crystal clear' portrays the purity of Clear quartz crystal, which is the solidification of pure light.

hours he was excreting fluid almost by the pint and was nearly unconscious. By the time the doctor arrived his appendix was ruptured. It was up to me to wait for the ambulance or make a dash for the nearest hospital 25 miles away. I drove as fast as I have ever driven and delivered Stephen to the emergency team who were waiting the other end.

He was unconscious by this time. They put him immediately on to a drip feed. Then tests began. I waited in tense desperation while they decided what to do. The doctors said it might not be a ruptured appendix after all. He was showing many of the signs of kidney failure and might have to be put on a kidney machine. I asked how long the treatment would have to last.

'For the rest of his life,' they replied calmly.

Their calm continued. I wanted to scream. I was certain that the appendix had ruptured and that if they did not operate in a few minutes the child would be dead. Hours were like weeks as we waited for the results of the tests. It was evening before they confirmed that it was the appendix after all and took him into surgery. Mothers were not allowed in; so I went off in the hope of spending the couple of hours in my favourite corner of Lincoln Cathedral. There, I felt, I would find relative peace. The Cathedral, however, was closed. I sat in the only place still open: a fish and chip shop, idly picking at food from time to time and looking constantly at my watch.

I met the anaesthetist as they wheeled Stephen out of the surgery.

'It was a close shave. He's been very sick. But I think he will be all right now.'

I could have hugged him.

Stephen lay for days on end in his hospital bed, his little 11-year-old body wired up like a telephone exchange. He showed few signs of life, save only the breath which came and went as quietly as it does in sleep; and the gentle moans, calling for

'Mu-um' if ever I moved my hand away for a moment or two from his abdomen. When the morphine injections penetrated his muscles these cries escalated to gut-rending screams of agony. In this there was no choice: without the morphine the pain would have reached dangerously high levels. When the pain subsided he invariably returned to his semi-coma, looking for all the world as though that was where he intended to stay.

It was clear that, drugs and all other considerations aside, Stephen was in deep shock. He had, after all, been within a hair's breadth of losing his life; that is shock enough. He had also lost his home and all that had been familiar to him for most of his life. And then there was the surgeon's knife: this is a familiar part of modern life, and how wonderful that they can save our lives; but the knives are nevertheless experienced as an onslaught on our stunned bodies. I wondered how he might improve if the shock could be treated.

At the time I knew little about the phenomenon of shock: only that it was something whose profound effects were perhaps only fully recognized by practitioners of complementary therapies such as homoeopathy. I knew too that Vicky Wall had discovered more than most about shock thanks to her auric sight. She had been an ambulance driver during the war and gained the nickname 'Pegasus' because she had a reputation for an uncanny knack of appearing, like the winged horse of Greek mythology, at the scene of so many cases of extreme injury. She very often arrived at the moment of crisis. With her second sight she noticed a common feature of all the deaths or near-deaths: that as the life force began to leave the body it moved out below the left rib. This is illustrated in Plate 13.

The interesting thing was that even if the person recovered, the aura, or the energy field, frequently remained displaced, leading to a permanent imbalance in the whole of the energy flow of the body.

What was I to do? My training so far had taught me, in cases of shock, to massage the Shock bottle, the Orange over Orange, all down the left side of the body from the ear lobe to the ankle. This would bring the aura back into its correct position and seal up the gap. Here, however, I had a child who was still quite hard to get at. He barely wanted to move; if sat up he slumped down within minutes and returned to sleep; and even in good health he disliked the sensation of 'yucky oils' on his body. In addition to all this he was wired up to a drip. I looked for a more acceptable solution, and decided to work on the energetic field around him. I reached for an Orange '*Pomander*' which was one of Vicky Wall's concoctions: a herbal formula modified from the original inspiration for *Balance* especially for working off the body rather than on it. I poured some drops of this *Pomander* into the palm of my hand and rubbed my hands together, knowing from experience that this would sharpen my sensitivity to the energetic field around Stephen's body. As soon as I brought my hands near to his field, the heat and the tingling sensation began to spread through my palms and fingers. This was familiar enough. What was not familiar was to feel a powerful energy, almost like a wall, extending the entire length of the area to the left of his body way beyond the normal limit of the tangible auric sphere; and to feel an empty space to his right. The right side was lifeless. I spent half an hour sweeping the energy back from Stephen's left side towards the centre.

Wait for it ... This turned out to be one of the most exciting days of my life. Stephen was sitting up in a chair when I began. The experiment of sitting him up had been tried before without success: five minutes had exhausted his energy on a couple of previous occasions. Now, as I worked, I felt the energy field returning from the left side, to which it had been so heavily displaced, right back almost to the centre again. As this happened, he felt his physical energy flooding back as his body began to regain its balance.

After half an hour he asked me to stop: it was, he said, all back where it should be except for half an inch. He had had enough. We could do the rest later. This was reasonable enough in an 11-year-old who felt better enough to get on and do something when for days on end he had lain comatose. He went back to his bed. There he sat up and we played games, without any interruptions for sleep, for the next six hours! When finally I left with a friend to go home he was still sitting up in his bed, smiling and chatting.

The ward sister and the other nurses were curious at these unusual goings-on, and surprised by the consequences. I was astonished. Yet really this is not so extraordinary when we look at it in the light of modern physics, which we shall do in the next chapter.

It took some months to restore Stephen to full health. The warmth and comfort of the cottage made it an easier job than it would have been in the farmhouse. I sold my lifetime's collection of books to supplement the social security money on which we lived. This meant I could feed Stephen with all sorts of wonderful foods to build his body up again. There is an odd satisfaction in renunciation. I had no need of books and certainly no time to read them. I knew I could get some again later if I wanted any. I had abandoned my cheque book along with the marriage; and there was a simplicity in knowing that the few £10 notes which I fetched every week from the Post Office, courtesy of the Welfare State, represented our income. Our capital was our few possessions, such as the books, the few items of furniture which were ours, and a little jewellery, the value of which would come in useful later. We always had enough; and at times of crisis such as this there was invariably a way round.

So we settled down, after a fashion. I was increasingly fascinated by the colour work, and the intense healing experience with Stephen had focused my attention. Within a few months Stephen was fully recovered and coping courageously with the almost complete absence of his father. My elder daughter was resettled and happy at her old school in Oxford, thanks to a 'fairy godmother'. Magdalen, the youngest, was contented in her new warm bedroom. She needed constant companionship, but that was also what she gave. I was deeply weary, but I was grateful for these children. Every one of them was warm and loving and strong. I dared to hope that the apprenticeship was over and that soon I should find a context in which I could begin to use my various experiences in some helpful way.

I observed with some interest that the crisis with Stephen had been the first time in two years that we had experienced any emergency large or small without the help of Mike. Despite his busy schedule and his frequent absences in working abroad, he had always somehow or other appeared out of the blue in our times of greatest need – and these occasions had been numerous.

What had been the lessons until this point? Perhaps we could summarize the principal issues associated with the first three major energy centres. Within the base chakra we have the preoccupations with survival: food, warmth and shelter, often understood within Western society simply as money. There is also the anger and resentment which we have to deal with when attempts to overcome these and other difficulties are frustrated. The principal challenge within the Pink is around the need for the unconditional love which enables us to accept ourselves and grow. The Coral and the Orange contain the problems of dependency and co-dependency. The Gold and the Yellow point to fears on every level; to the issues around self-worth, and the challenge of becoming ourselves.

So how do these relate to the experience we had been living? Well, for one thing we had survived. Stephen was still alive; and with a smaller income than anyone I knew we were happier than we had ever been. I remembered a friend once saying to me years before that everyone should go through the experience of losing everything at least once; and for the first time I began to understand what she had meant.

Then there are the issues of finding love and acceptance for ourselves; and the ones of dependency and co-dependency. I had left a marriage which had been held together, like so many, by threads more of fear than of love: the need for security, the fear of being alone, the need to be needed. I had left behind me this dependent/co-dependent relationship. Had I not, however, to some extent transferred this dependency on to Mike? I saw him not only as a doctor, a healer and a teacher, but also as the provider of solutions. It had not yet occurred to me that I could quite well manage without another person to advise and lead me, even despite the fact that I had carried most of the responsibility for the children and the practical details of daily life alone for the previous 17 years. I was still addicted to the idea that someone would share my responsibilities. I had yet to understand that in working with me Mike was giving me back to myself.

On this last occasion Mike had been abroad, and I had not only coped alone, but discovered that I could have a considerable influence on the process of Stephen's recovery without someone else's magic touch. I recalled the words which a dear friend had so often repeated to me in the past: 'You must take back your power.' Not knowing that I had ever had any power to lose in the first place, I had found it hard to understand what he meant.

So then the Yellow: the discovery of the individual self, separate from the group, yet intimately connected with it. Like every other human being, I must have some unique quality to contribute. What I had needed was to find the courage to be myself; to listen to my own inner voice instead of the outer voice of authority. Maybe I had needed to move away from a state of dependency before I could begin to discover who I was and what it was that I was here for.

The imbalances which tend to occur within these chakras before we find the inner harmony which frees us to move on are universal: at this point in the history of humanity most people's attention is focused upon these concerns. This is well understood by those engaged in advertising, who attract our attention by reference to our desire for security, our yearning to possess, our need to feel attractive, our desire for sexual gratification, our need to feel part of a group, our tendency to look outside ourselves for approval, our frail sense of our own value, our desire to feed and boost the ego.

It is not only advertisers who feed off these universal difficulties and fears. The arms trade thrives upon our unresolved difficulties within the lower chakras: survival, and other Red issues, such as aggression; and Yellow ones, such as power. Money lenders tempt us with perpetual offers of happiness based upon possession: another Red issue. Insurance companies depend for their living upon our various anxieties around survival and security. The illegal drugs trade exploits dependency issues, particularly of one of the most vulnerable groups in society: the young. Manufacturers of commercial goods depend largely upon a climate of competition rather than co-operation. The tabloid press flourishes upon our appetite for 'news' which feeds our fears and boosts our fragile confidence. We feel a welcome, if false, sense of security in the illusion that a distant misfortune or misdemeanour affirms our security or substantiates our own worthiness.

The challenge for us all is to overcome these obstacles from within: to provide our own sense of security and strength; to let go of our need to judge ourselves and others; to find that place inside ourselves which is of love instead of fear. Then we shall have no need to live on one another's fears, and the focus of our energy can change direction, towards activity and thought which is essentially creative, and which thus nurtures ourselves and all those with whom we interact.

'We shall know that mankind is awakening beyond these chakras,' Mike suggested to a group, 'when we see an advertisement for a sports car with a nun sitting on the bonnet ...'

That is doubtless still a long way off, but meanwhile we can continue the journey upwards towards the heart. At present our hearts, so often wounded, are focused upon the need for emotional food. As we awaken, the heart can open in a new way. It can become the vehicle for the discovery of our own truth, and the expression of truth, and of love. We can stretch out to reach others on a new level. The next stage of the journey presents us with exciting opportunities as we meet the challenge to rise above our basic concerns and grow towards our full humanity.

When, as individuals, we find the wisdom to recognize ourselves and to value the gift of our humanity, then perhaps mankind can let mankind into his heart. We can leave behind the divisiveness which comes from fear, and learn to communicate, from individual to individual and nation to nation.

Let us look first at what we can begin to understand about the energetic workings of the universe, since the comprehension of this may lead us towards a new awareness of the part that each of us has to play.

LIVING ENERGIES

Every living organism emanates an 'aura' or a field of energy extending outwards from the physical body. Or, we could look at this the other way around: we could say that every physical body, whether that of a tree or a flower, an animal or a person, is the *product* of the aura which surrounds it. It all depends on our point of view; and it seems to me that in the light of modern knowledge that point of view is changing fast.

How can the application of colour affect the condition of the aura or of the physical body? How could the sweeping of the Orange energy from my hands possibly have such a radical effect on the physical condition of a child in deep shock? Because really, however we may explain it, that event *was* very extraordinary. In working partly with my training, but predominantly with my instinct, I suddenly had confirmation that my previously held world view, the certainty of which I had doubted for some time, was definitely out of date.

BEINGS OF LIGHT
It is way beyond the scope of this book to explore the nature of the universe as given to us by contemporary science.

Nevertheless, hold on to your seats and please stay tuned: I cannot resist a little bit of theory …

Colour therapy in this form has only existed for around 14 years. When Vicky Wall first offered the *Balance* bottles to the world as the cornerstone of a system which might restore the flow of our energies and bring harmony to minds and bodies, many of us still retained in our minds the Newtonian model of the universe offered to us at school: a universe consisting essentially of matter divided by space. We believed that we each sat, for example, in our own separate and solid chair which supported the weight of our bodies, each of which was complete, and separate from the next one. A safe and respectable space kept these bodies, whether people or chairs, each at an appropriate distance from the next. For a while the world seemed unchanging and predictable; reliable and solid. Isaac Newton was born in 1642 and lived until 1727, by which time he was widely considered as the father of a science which was total and absolute. His main work, published over 300 years ago, established the foundations of all 'classical' physics, and in a world which was less obviously subject to constant change than that of the twentieth century, his philosophy was widely accepted as gospel truth for at least two and a half centuries. Yet Newton himself knew by the end of his life that his work was merely the very beginning. He wrote:

> I do not know what I may appear to the world, but to myself I seem to have been only like a boy playing on the sea-shore, and diverting myself in now and then finding a smoother pebble or a prettier shell than ordinary, while the great ocean of truth lay all undiscovered before me.

Universal law is inexorable: one of the things which it states is the inevitability of change. The world is not solid and constant. All things are in a state of constant flow, constant movement, constant evolution. Moment to moment, all is in a state of perpetual change and motion. Perhaps this is easier for us to perceive at this time in history, as we drive around in our cars, bombarded at every turn with physical evidence of the constant movement of energy. From our cars we can perceive the universe as a kaleidoscope. Everywhere we see the coming and going of vehicles, the glow and the flashing of lights, the movement of people, the exchange of information; and our ears experience the energy of sound. Every moment is different from the last, never to be exactly reproduced. This is merely the outer manifestation of the secret life of the earth and the universe itself, where every atom is vibrating with life, movement and change: each crystal, each flower, each person condensing and transmitting the energy of light in its own unique manner. For this is the reality which Einstein began to discover during his lifetime until his death in 1952, paving the way for a radically new world view. How very different from the apparent and reassuring stability of the seventeenth- and eighteenth-century world, with its quiet movement of horses and carts.

With the inevitability of change, Einstein offered us the quantum theory of radiation, and relativity; and in his wake there have followed several generations of nuclear physicists whose findings have turned the old order upside-down. Little by little science has gained access to that 'great ocean of truth', to discover a new and very different reality.

Here is one aspect of that new reality: Newton's contemporary, Robert Hooke, had opposed Newton's corpuscular theory of light with a wave theory. The discoveries of the twentieth century have revealed that neither theory was complete: light behaves both as a particle *and* as a wave.

Furthermore, as nuclear physics evolved, the first and the most important form of energy became recognized as being the energy of light. Light is the primary, original, energy of the universe; the building block of creation.

Vicky Wall had recognized this from the very beginning of *Balance*. She had birthed this system through inspiration, after a lifetime's work as a pharmacist and chiropodist. Vicky had been endowed all her life with considerable clairvoyant powers as well as a profound gift for healing. She was asked from time to time whether she had done any 'research'. She replied that she had been taken back to the beginning when God said, 'Let there be light'. She wrote: 'And there was light. And light was the life force and the beginning of the life energies, and there I "re-searched" and thus, remembering, entered the mysterious and magical world of colour in the Greater Garden of God.'

From the very beginning, Vicky was encapsulating, in putting together the *Balance* bottles, the energies of light. She was not a nuclear physicist; the limit of her scientific training was as a pharmacist. But she *knew*. She knew that colour is light. She was given a formula, not only for bringing together different aspects of that light, but also for potentizing the package once assembled. She was shown how she might bring the energies from another dimension through to this one in a way which would be helpful for mankind. So each bottle would be a veritable power pack, bringing the light force into healing. While the full implications of this were not apparent to Vicky at once, her intuition was active from the first, opening her to receive whatever insights might later be revealed.

White light, when it is divided through a prism, breaks into the seven colours of the rainbow. It divides further into an infinity of shades and tints. On the night that *Balance* was born, Vicky saw waves of colour moving towards her; as she reached for them they receded. With years of pharmaceutical knowledge behind her she recaptured them, bringing together the energies of plants and crystals and gems: she 'balanced' brilliantly coloured oils with their essences over equally astonishing colours of herbal waters to make a completely new form of healing package in a system whose language is colour. She knew little about what it meant, or where this was all leading: she followed her powerful intuition and allowed something extraordinary to come through her.

The depth and the breadth and the mystery of this reality – the reality which Vicky 're-searched' – is not easy to condense into any kind of book. The energies of light are more easily grasped by experience than by reason. Nevertheless, they have been revered and to some extent understood in the East for thousands of years. As science reunites with spiritual awareness, after a rift of so many centuries, many more clues are offered. Some of the mysteries of the universe are beginning to be revealed. Therefore, it seems inevitable that science and spiritual thought are joining forces. What an exciting time to be on earth!

When God said 'Let there be light', this heralded the beginning of the created world: the appearance of light from the darkness of the void. Light is essential to our existence here on earth. The smallest building block of life is light and exists in light. While the sun was not the *source* of life on earth, it was the catalyst for the appearance of life on earth. Without the light of the sun, nothing would survive for an instant. It provides a cycle of energy: the earth is sustained by light, which it converts into food. Food and warmth together sustain us. More subtly we are fed by light directly through our skin and our eyes.

Creation did not just happen once: it is a continuous process. The universe which was once understood as being composed of matter divided by space is now seen as one enormous field of energy, of varying concentrations. This energy is composed of light.

Here I would offer a highly simplified version of a scientific truth which is vastly complex: the light energy gradually lowers itself in vibration, becoming denser, and finally condensing itself to form the physical world.

The realization of this fundamental fact turns our established world upside-down. The logical consequence is that even our old armchairs are condensed light... And so the light continues to come to earth, causing miracles of creation at every moment. St Francis's almond tree is one dramatic demonstration of the bursting of the creative force as season follows season and light comes to earth.

Once we accept this premise there follows an astonishing conclusion: we, as part of the physical world, come directly from the source of light; and if the building block of all creation is light, we must ourselves be *composed* of light. We are light! This idea, which is new to many of us, has been recognized for at least 2000 years in the East. Within the philosophy of acupuncture it has long been taught that the aura, or the energy field surrounding the physical body, *creates* that body.

This is not all. It gets more and more astounding. The logical conclusion of all this is that we have a light body *before* we have a physical body. It is a kind of etheric blueprint for what will become the body. This is one aspect of a universal law which comes up quite frequently in working with colour. In *Aura-Soma* we express this law in the phrase: 'Energy follows thought'. The blueprint, the idea, the thought form comes first and only then does it manifest as something we can see and touch.

This means, for one thing, that we had better be careful what we think, as it may happen! Have you ever heard the cautionary tale about the couple who longed so desperately for a white Rolls-Royce that they got one through their front window...? It also means that we may make sense of phenomena such as absent healing: healing energy in this connection is the manifestation of *thought*. This may be given in the conventionally accepted sense of prayer. It may also be given as colour in the minds of those who are giving the healing. All colour is living energy, in whatever form, shape or substance; and therefore even colour used in thought contains a resonance of the living energy which is its source.

So, to look further at this model, or this scientific truth which explains the universe as condensed light, as the light moves nearer and nearer to our physical bodies, so it becomes more concentrated. The physical body is thus the most concentrated part of our own energy field, which extends infinitely outwards, overlapping and co-existing with everything else: with the energy fields of people and animals and trees. So it all keeps coming back to colour: life is energy; energy is light; light is colour; colour is movement; movement is life.

Once the physical body is created the movement continues. There is two-way traffic between the subtle and the physical levels, the subtle bodies continuously nourishing and energizing the physical, and the physical repercussing upon the whole of the aura. Proper care and nurturing of the physical body keeps the energetic body, as well as the physical, vital and robust. Conversely any abuse of the physical caused through pollution, undue stress, drugs or alcohol, for example, will cause the auric field to become depleted. The entire auric field consists of a number of different levels: beyond the physical level there are six more, subtle, bodies. It is sufficient here to say that these realms include the emotional, the mental and the spiritual bodies, all of whose state of health will inevitably repercuss upon the physical. There is an intimate and certain relationship between all the different levels of the being, from the physical right through to the spiritual: just as an imbalance in one level will affect all the others, so the feeding of any one aspect will also foster the health and vitality of the whole system.

So what about Stephen and the radical recovery of his energy flow? Why, for one thing, was his physical energy completely blocked when the auric field had shifted off centre? Well, one of the first laws of light is that it travels in straight lines. It is not very good at turning corners. So if the whole of the auric body moves off centre, shifting way over to the left, the flow of the universal energy or the life force will have a problem in reaching the physical body.

Many people are vaguely aware that some event in their lives triggered off a train of ill health. This is a phenomenon so well recognized by homoeopaths that it even has a name: it is known as an NBWS, which stands for 'Never Been Well Since'. Something which has happened has acted as a trigger for an imbalance which has never subsequently righted itself. Frequently, this event is some kind of shock or trauma. This is not necessarily a near death experience or a severe illness: frequently the trigger can be a mental or emotional shock which may not even have struck us at the time as being particularly significant. In all these cases, however, it is the *energetic* imbalance which must be redressed; without this a person may drag the uneven energy flow with them throughout the rest of their lives, never recovering full health. Indeed, it is even possible that the energetic result of such trauma may be brought through to a subsequent incarnation, resulting in a lop-sided energy field which is detectable from the very beginning of that person's life.

So now we are beginning to see a model for our existence as human beings which moves a long way beyond the relatively straightforward solid body which we can see and touch and feel. All is energy. Nothing is static. Existence implies the movement of energy, and furthermore this is the very basis of relationship. As part of the created world, we are involved in a continuous relationship with all that is.

EXPANSION

In birthing and working with *Aura-Soma*, Vicky Wall had clearly intuited much of the knowledge which is now becoming more available to us through science: the living, moving energies of which we and our universe are comprised.

For some years *Balance*, the emulsion which is applied directly on the physical body, worked alone. Vicky Wall knew that *Balance* on its own was capable of accessing the full healing response. There came a time, however, when she felt that people sometimes wanted a quicker response; that *Balance* could perhaps be supported by something even more.

Since early childhood Vicky had made a habit of collecting herbs and studying their medicinal properties. At the time that she was beginning to wonder about extending the way in which *Aura-Soma* could work, she noticed that her lifetime's collection of herbs had reached the magical number of 49: seven times seven. Man as a being of light has seven chakras and seven bodies; Vicky, like some others with clairvoyant sight, was the seventh child of a seventh child. It has been known at least since Pythagoras that numbers carry energy. Forty-nine, she knew, was a special number, and she took it as a sign. She took the herbs and combined them in a new way.

We have seen an illustration of this new way in action, in the case of recalling Stephen from a state of deep shock. So what exactly are these concoctions by means of which we can work so effectively on the auric level?

THE POMANDERS

Vicky Wall's new formula involved not oils or herbal waters, but herbs preserved and presented in a base of alcohol, which evaporates into the aura. The word *Pomander* originated with the use of an apple, 'pomme' in French, studded with cloves to purify the atmosphere and assist the judges in making clear decisions in court.

Vicky devised and taught a simple way whereby these *Pomanders* could be applied by the hands directly on to the aura. Three drops are put into the palm of the left hand, the palms of the hands themselves being minor chakras; the hands are then rubbed together and the arms and hands stretched upwards. This allows the alcohol content to evaporate, and signifies the intention to share all healing energy before accepting it for ourselves. 'Energy follows thought': the rays are offered for the healing of the planet, after which the hands work gently around the crown, the back of the head, and down the front of the body through all the energy centres in an action similar to physical massage, except only that the hands remain at a distance of several inches from the body. Finally the hands are brought back to the face and the *Pomander* is inhaled in three deep breaths. In doing this we are providing the body with several routes by which the *Pomander* may be absorbed: through the skin, directly through the aura, and through the breath. If we are offering a treatment with a *Pomander* to someone else, we can work around the whole of the body, back and front.

Why might this way, the treating of the energetic field, answer people's need for a *quicker* response? We might suppose that further away from the body would, more likely, mean slower.

After the day of treating Stephen's shock with the Orange *Pomander*, I was offered still more revelations. During his convalescence, working with my hands on Stephen's abdomen, I had for a while focused on maintaining a movement of energy in order to break down the adhesions which were likely to form within the gut. All was going well and he was thoroughly comforted by the presence of warm hands. Yet after a while something prompted me to move my hands nine or ten inches away from his body. Stephen's response was immediate. Where, before, he had merely experienced comfort and warmth and some degree of relief from his pain, he now exclaimed in surprise:

'Keep your hands like that!'

He had felt immediately the physical movement deep inside the gut, which he described as a feeling of things becoming unstuck. Yet, it had only been when I removed my hands from physical contact and begun to work from an auric level that he experienced this response from within.

When we really start to think about this it makes sense. Let us look again at the energetic workings of the Universe, as presented some pages back. According to this model, remember, light energy lowers itself in vibration to create the physical world. The highest vibrations, quite simply, are very very fast. The lower ones are slower. Therefore, in the subtle regions energies move fast; in this fast movement they can bring about quicker change. The physical realms are denser and therefore slower to move.

It is interesting to reflect in connection with this that, of all the planets in outer space, Pluto has the furthest distance from earth. It is so far away that it was not even discovered until a few decades ago. Yet its influence, according to many astrologers, upon the earth and its inhabitants is possibly more powerful than that of any other planet.

In recognizing the vital importance, literally, of maintaining the energetic body in a healthy state of repair, Vicky formulated the *Pomanders* not only with the knowledge that through the aura we could feed the system fast with whatever ray is needed the most. She also recognized our need for protection at the energetic level.

This is because our bodies, indeed our whole systems, are not quite as solid and material as we once thought they were! Part of the consequence of inhabiting an ever-moving field of energy is that we constantly interact with the fields of those around us. We, and they, frequently overflow. This means that we can sometimes become depleted: unconsciously we may give our energy away. We may also, from time to time, absorb a quality of energy which is not especially compatible with our own. Neither of these situations is conducive to the optimum balance of our vital force. It is helpful to maintain a kind of energetic integrity, and for this the *Pomanders* are very effective.

The earth is surrounded by a protective layer of blue energy, which safeguards its surface from being fried by the harmful rays from the sun. Similarly, we need protection from the daily stresses of living which can cause small gaps or weaknesses in the aura. If we treat someone with a *Pomander* we can often feel these weak areas; one of the immediate effects of using a *Pomander* is to heighten our own sensitivity to the energetic field around ourselves and others. Frequently, these weak areas are experienced in treatment as a sensation of cold on our own hands. We can generally remedy this in a short time by concentrating on bringing the colour ray which the person needs most to that area of weakness. Kirlian photographs have shown the film of protection provided by a *Pomander* as a bar surrounding the aura, and containing little valves which filter out all negative energies, but which allow positive energies to enter. All positive vibrations enhance the strength of our auric field.

When we apply a *Pomander* around the energetic field, therefore, we are enhancing a particular colour ray and covering ourselves with a warm cloak of protection, ready for all weathers, so to speak.

The best way to understand any of this is to experiment in using *Pomanders*. People experience many different sensations when using them, and the most helpful thing that any of us can do is to try and see – or feel. As with *Balance*, we are led to the most appropriate *Pomander* by our colour choice. More exactly, it is the process of examining our selection of *Balance* bottles which will lead us to such a *Pomander*. A liking for the fragrance is then a useful confirmation, or otherwise, of whether we have found the most suitable choice. Each *Pomander* contains all of the 49 precious herbs which Vicky chose and assembled over the years, in varying proportions according to the chakra to which they are addressed. Currently there are 14 different *Pomanders*. The subtle variations in their colour, and in the heavenly smell which emanates from them once the lid is removed, reflect the subtle gradations through the chakra system of the body.

Several of the *Pomanders* have some unexpected side-effects. The White one, for example, is not only a powerful disinfectant but also has the capacity for drawing together flesh which has been wounded, so enormously speeding up the healing process in cuts large or small. For this reason some dentists who have learnt of *Aura-Soma* are using it to cauterize wounds in the mouth (it tastes horrible!). The Magenta one helps to stabilize the energy received in treatment by acupuncture: applied to a point directly after the needle has been removed, it prolongs the effect. The Orange one has the astounding capacity for restoring the tired or obstinate engines of cars or computers which are unwilling to start. It does not always work, but I have witnessed several occasions when it has.

Aura-Soma, along with Vicky's understanding, was expanding and deepening. The colours had begun to travel to far-flung corners of the earth, returning to Vicky with messages of astonishment and joy. Guided by her intuition, and energized by the ever-increasing wealth of information which she received from people who used *Balance* and the *Pomanders* with startling results, she decided to go a step further. She 'birthed' a range of 15 bottles which for the most part contained very much paler colours than the earlier ones. These are now known as the 'Master' range of bottles. In her constant intercourse with the higher dimensions she had come to feel that there was a point beyond which colour takes on a personality. The paler the tint, the nearer it was to the light from the Source. Each colour, she felt, reflected at very high levels a particular aspect of the source of pure White light. She believed that if we were to make a connection with a particular ray or rays we would open ourselves to receive a specific quality of energy, or guidance, from the Source. She decided, therefore, that the new bottles should each have a name. She related each bottle to the energy of an Ascended Master, a highly evolved being existing in spirit. These bottles seemed to confirm Vicky's intuition in the quality of energy which they offered. Both the quality of information which the choice of any of them revealed, and the effect they could have in producing a healing response, appeared to reach new levels. It was as though the entire process was moving up to a new level of vibration. The energy radiating from substances may be measured by radionics machines. These are computer-like boxes which can both track with acute accuracy the imbalances throughout the different areas of the body, and energize water or salts to provide remedies highly specific to each individual. They can also measure the energies radiated by people or other living objects. Such measurements confirm that the energy level of these 'Master' bottles is more potent than that of the others.

Before long, therefore, Vicky found it was time to access this new dimension in the concoctions she produced for the aura. *Balance* was applied on the skin, the *Pomanders* were applied to the electromagnetic field – that field of energy directly surrounding and close to the physical body. It seemed to Vicky that there was still room for something more: the quintessential formula had still to be found before the system would be complete. And so came the next stage of the process.

THE QUINTESSENCES

What Vicky put together now looked similar to the *Pomanders*: collections of herbs in an alcohol base. Just as the Master range of *Balance* bottles are paler than the rest, so too the *Quintessences* are paler than the *Pomanders*. They are also more potent.

The *Quintessences* are the subtlest of all the products in the *Aura-Soma* range. They may be compared to flower essences, or to high potency homoeopathics: diluted and ethereal. This means that, rather than acting on the denser bodies, they do their work right out in the subtle realms. Like the *Pomanders*, the *Quintessences* are swept through the aura; but from the wrists rather than the hands. This is because there is an energy channel connecting the wrists directly with the heart. The *Quintessence* energy, while gentle like all the energies of colour, is deeply and powerfully penetrating.

Whereas the *Pomanders* are recommended for frequent use, giving constant protection and reinforcement to the aura, the *Quintessences* have a different function. Their energy may be harnessed at any time when we wish to invoke a quality, or a particular energy, from a higher level of vibration. In doing this we may bring into the auric sphere the most creative aspect of the colour to which each *Quintessence* relates. This may be when we wish to work actively on a particular aspect of our growth: before meditation, for example, or while working to develop a quality such as commitment, compassion, or a sense of peace. They may also be used at the beginning of specific projects where a particular quality of energy might enhance the process. This might be the creative expression from the heart, for example, when we are writing or producing a play; or it might be the search for clear sound judgement in a difficult legal case.

As with the *Pomanders*, the best way to understand the *Quintessences* is to use them ourselves. People become acquainted with the energies of *Quintessences* through very many different experiences and sensations. Some, at first, experience little more than a tingling sensitivity in the tips of the fingers as soon as a few drops are placed on the wrist. Some will feel a forceful sense of grounding, the energy fairly rushing through them as their feet become aware of the earth below them. A lot depends, of course, upon which *Quintessence* they are using at the time. Another person, using a different *Quintessence*, may discover a gentle boost to their creative energy as blocks become dissolved and poetry, long buried, emerges through their pen; or canvasses come to life in response to the brushing of their paint.

In *Aura-Soma* courses time is given to the mutual exchange of the energy of *Pomanders* and *Quintessences* in a specific routine of massaging the aura and enhancing the energy flow. This technique, once learned, is taken and used by many therapists as a powerful and gentle support to the consultations brought about through *Balance*.

With the powerful energetic support given to *Balance* by the *Pomanders* and the *Quintessences*, *Aura-Soma* was by now a complete and unique system whereby we might find the remedy for many pains and problems; and, above all, whereby we might subtly alter our consciousness in order to perceive and create a gentler reality.

As our understanding grows, and our consciousness expands, we can begin to grasp the reality that we live in a universe in which all is interconnected.

COSMIC CONNECTIONS

To work with *Pomanders* and *Quintessences*, feeling something of the powerful energies which affect us from the subtle realms, is to begin to experience an important reality – according to natural law everything is connected, originating from and returning to the same source.

Human beings and animals and trees and plants and even the Earth herself are bound together by the commonness of our origin. Therefore, every act which we perform towards another we perform also towards ourselves. Everything receives and transmits something of the universal life force in a perpetual moving flow of energy. The destruction of the rain forests in Ecuador or Brazil will influence the whole of the planetary climate; an earth tremor in Tokyo will, in some infinitely subtle way, affect the leaves of the trees in a London park; the thought of loving kindness in the heart of Mother Teresa raises the vibration throughout the planet towards greater light, where the thoughts of Hitler once lowered that vibration towards the darkness.

By the same token, our own thoughts create an energy

which will, inevitably, have some subtle effect on the rest of the universe. It is for us to choose whether that energy is positive or negative. Do we wish to create, or to destroy? As we get in touch with our own colours, we can bring more of our thoughts to the conscious mind, and thence begin to take responsibility for their quality. For we are not passive entities, buffeted about by forces beyond our control: each of us plays a vital part in an unfolding drama as the history of the world moves onward. We are individuals, each one unique, and each with more power than we ever knew. To recognize our colours is to recognize who we really are; to become conscious of the nature of our intentions and our thoughts. Then we can take back the power which we never knew we had lost; we can realize the possibility of bringing that power into the world in order to become co-creators with the Divine. That is our destiny.

TELEPATHY

This fact, that all is energy and therefore somehow interlinked, is something which is instinctively understood by children and animals, and less easily understood as we 'mature' and our rational minds overwhelm and dominate our natural sensitivity. What about telepathy, for example? The first time I experienced a clear example of this was shortly before I left Oxford. Magdalen was a tiny baby requiring full-time care, and I was suffering from a fever so high that I could scarcely find the strength to turn over in bed. My husband not being someone who could handle babies or illness, I was alone and very alarmed for Magdalen's welfare. When the phone rang it was a close friend who was living in Florida. We had not been in contact for some weeks.

'Don't worry, darling,' said a familiar voice from 3,000-odd miles away. 'I just wanted to let you know I'm thinking of you. You will soon be better.'

Is this some special gift given only to a chosen few? I don't believe that this is at all the case. Have you ever noticed that when you have been thinking a lot about someone close to you they will ring up or write? This is not really as surprising as it may have seemed. Our thoughts travel at the speed of lightning because that is what they are! My daughter Nicola tells me she has given up bothering to say much to me because as her thoughts form I express them before she has had time to speak.

It is helpful to contemplate, in this connection, our dual nature as beings of light. If light is capable of behaving both as a particle and as a wave, it follows that this too is our own capability. The particle aspect of ourselves is that which has form and substance: while this form and substance is in a constant state of flux, it is nevertheless easily recognized as the physical body of the being. It is limited by time and space, and it is grounded and linked with the earth. The wave aspect of ourselves is that aspect which has no form or substance perceptible to the normal senses; and it is not limited by time or space. In other words it can be everywhere at once. So we are, in some sense, simultaneously sitting at our office desk and travelling the universe, as particles and as waves. The signature of both the particles and the waves is their colour.

ANIMALS

We can learn a lot from our pets. When I departed with my family from our downgrade farmhouse, circumstances compelled me to leave the dog with my ex-husband, who was fond of her. While I visited her and walked her reasonably frequently, I was careful never to bring her to the house where we were living, in order not to cause more confusion for the poor dog than was already inevitable. She had already lost her real owner Nicola, my eldest daughter who had gone away to boarding-school. They were devoted to each other. On the first occasion that I drove from our new home to bring Nicola back for a weekend in the cottage, which was some weeks after we had first moved in, we returned to find the dog sitting on the front doorstep, having negotiated three-quarters of a mile to get there. How had she known either where we lived, or that Nicola would be coming home that day?

No doubt many animal owners could cite similar examples. Those creatures who are not alienated by technology from the natural world are able very easily to communicate by telepathy, which is, after all, communication through a kind of natural universal telecommunications network which bypasses satellites and wires. The universe is energy. And, to remind ourselves once more why this has to do with colour – energy is light, and light is colour. Telepathy aside, animals, who by their nature are uncluttered by knowledge and the intellect, are very responsive to healing through colour. Unable, perhaps, to select colour for themselves, they must rely upon our intuition as their friends.

THE DARK SIDE OF THE BRAIN

Everything is energy. We need to recognize and absorb the truth of this statement, because it has all sorts of implications. The world, and the whole universe, is energy rather than solid matter; and when we accept the implications of this fact we can begin to redress an imbalance which has existed for hundreds of years.

The name '*Balance*' can be looked at on several levels, beyond the physical and beyond the individual. All dis-ease is imbalance at one level or another. We experience frequent imbalances as individuals, but it goes further than this. A state of imbalance can affect whole societies and civilizations.

We are just moving out of one Age, the Age of Pisces, and into a new one, the Age of Aquarius. An Age lasts, on average, around two and a half thousand years, and each one has its characteristic flavour. Like everything else, it has strengths and weaknesses. One of the distinguishing marks of the Age of Pisces has been patriarchy. The evidence seems to be that this has manifested as an imbalance on a large scale. It is not simply a question of domination by men; that is only a part of it. The essence of this imbalance, or tipping of the scales, is something far deeper. It is an unevenness in the balance of two complementary forces, the masculine and the feminine, within each of us. The masculine force is essentially an outgoing, rational, analytical force while the feminine is the receptive, intuitive, creative one.

So what have we been doing for a few hundred or thousand years? We have looked outside ourselves for authority; we have bowed to the masculine in others and in ourselves. We have tended towards whatever is rational, measurable, visible or in some way immediately available to the senses and our logical mind. For a very long time, we have valued and trusted the outer; that which has structure and form. In doing so we have built up a formidable technological empire, overcoming many of the fundamental problems and discomforts associated with physical survival. All this is quite an achievement. We have largely accomplished our external quest.

But there is a problem. Have we, perhaps, forgotten why we are here? Is it possible that the very competence with which we have harnessed our masculine energy, the logical, orderly way in which we have learned to dominate our environment and our nature, has created a sense of separation? In our isolation have we looked, for guidance or blame, to doctors and priests and outer teachers; the government, and even the weather – towards anything, in other words, rather than ourselves? In the symphony of bureaucracy which we have created, it seems, we have drowned the sounds of nature, and of the still small voice within.

What is this still small voice? It is our in-tuition; the inner teacher. It is the other half of ourselves. It is linked to the 'dark', unexplored side of the brain: the right side which in many people, for a long time, has lain dormant. The left brain, the rational analytical side of the brain, has been largely left in charge. It has been left in charge to such an extent that the right shoulder and the right side of the body have become larger than the left. At present the difference is subtle, but it is there.

So we need to redress the balance. We need to get back in touch with the inner: our femininity, our inner wisdom, our willingness to listen and receive. When we recognize our true colours it is exactly this dimension to which we are gaining access. To listen to our own inner voice is to find our own strength as individuals: then we have less need for any reference to guidance outside ourselves. We do not have to be victims any more. We can learn to take responsibility for ourselves!

We have seen that energy is universal, and that we are comprised of and fed by the universal life force. It all sounds so simple. So why are we not all the same? What is it that makes each of us individual? I will reduce the infinite mysteries of the universe to a simple formula: what it is that differs between one individual and another is the *quality* of energy. We receive and transmit the energies of light from the universe; and we then act as a kind of transformer of energy. The way in which we transform that energy is reflected in the quality of the light, or the *colour*, which we radiate. As all matter is energy vibrating at different rates, everything has its own distinctive wavelength.

'She is right on my wavelength'; 'I get good vibes around that person'. Again, the instinctive knowledge of this phenomenon is written into our language. We know who we feel comfortable with. Literally, this is because our vibrations are similar enough for us to recognize each other.

None of this is new. With the rediscovery of the

fundamental importance of the energies of colour and light, really what is happening is that we are getting back into touch with our essential nature. Light has been the building block of creation since the dawn of time.

We talk about the light of understanding. We hope to solve problems by bringing light into the situation. *Aura-Soma* works consciously with the energies of light. Just as, when we shine pure white light through a prism, the light is broken up into the colours of the rainbow, so *Aura-Soma* shines that light, those colours, on whatever problem or situation is brought to it. This means not only that we can see and understand the situation clearly, but through the precise nature of the colour we can analyse it into its component parts. It does this through the colours chosen by each person who comes to it. As Vicky Wall would so often say: 'You are the colours you choose, and the colours you choose reflect your being's needs.'

Given that we are predominantly unconscious beings (even Einstein was said to be possibly 10 per cent conscious on a good day…), the work of self-discovery can, in the normal run of things, be a long job. The exciting thing about colour is its direct reflection of ourselves at a deeper level than we might imagine possible: the level of pure consciousness. When we are offered the opportunity of choosing from these bottles those colour combinations which draw us most irresistibly towards themselves, we have the possibility of recognizing ourselves, not on an outer level or the level of personality, but from a place of pure consciousness. It is, in some mysterious and profound way, like standing in front of a mirror. Just as the eyes are the windows of the soul, so the colours are its mirror. Through our encounters with *Balance* we can transcend the limitations of personality and recognize our purest essence. This means that self-discovery may not have to be such a long job after all.

An encounter with the living, glowing, translucent energies

of *Balance* can stir deep down in the embers of our being some forgotten memory of another age, a brighter consciousness. Is it possible that as we enter this new era, this time of alteration in our consciousness, we are regaining something of our original understanding? Maybe what is stirring in the depths of ourselves when we encounter these colours is something very ancient: a re-membering of ourselves in our original and purest form.

Let us imagine that at the very beginning we set out on a journey from the source of pure White light. On the journey we encountered darkness and confusion; we lost our way. Yet surely this was all part of the plan. As on a treasure hunt, we had to search for clues. We journeyed in order to gain experience and wisdom; in order to grow. The lines etched on our faces are the lines of our lives, the paths of our experience. We have the potential to move through the darkness and confusion; to accept the difficulty as the means to greater wealth. Then, perhaps, we may find a clarity which is the greater for the lessons we have learned. Finally, at the end of a long voyage, we may exist as pure colour in perfect balance throughout all the levels of our being: rainbow beings of pure light in perfect balance and harmony. Perhaps part of the process was to forget, for a while, who we were; then what we needed was a gentle reminder, something which would enable us to 're-member' or to reunite all the scattered members of our fragmented consciousness which once balanced and combined might bring us to the fullness of who we may become. To allow this to happen is to realize our potential in its fullest form.

Are these lofty claims? I don't think so. The most profound solutions are often the simplest ones. In one sense colour is so simple. Colour, simply, *is*. We might have been called human doings, but we were not: we were created as human *beings*, relating to all that is. As human beings, we are here to learn.

Perhaps colour has been given to us in this new form at a time when we are prepared to awaken in a new way. And so, as we leave behind one or two of the preoccupations which locked us into the difficulties connected with our lower nature, we can continue the adventure, and journey towards the heart.

OLIVE GREEN

With the Olive Green comes the finding of the path towards the heart. The Olive Green area lies between the solar plexus and the region of the heart, protecting and supporting the heart from below.

With the Olive, also, comes the introduction of a new colour: the Yellow remains, but within it to form the Olive is the addition of Blue. Blue has a lot to do with communication. The combination of Olive Green is two parts Yellow to one part Blue: it is where we begin to bring the Yellow energy into use in a new way. It is the bringing of the wisdom and knowledge into the world; it is the communication of that wisdom.

The discovery and release of our individuality within the Yellow is incomplete until we use that individuality in a way which contributes to the whole. 'No man is an island.' The Olive is the beginning of a context in which the individuality of self may be brought into the shared space of the world, and communicated to others.

Olive is a ray which has long remained cloaked and hidden away. One of its main associations in the minds of many is with army uniforms, where one of its chief purposes is camouflage.

In *Aura-Soma* its first appearance among the *Balance* bottles was in bottle number 91, just over four years ago. It is a colour which has remained in the residential bank of the source of colours for many many millennia, and remained comparatively unnoticed until recently. It must have been there since the very dawn of time, since its vibration is exactly that of the world of nature: its energies are everywhere evident in the creation of the leaves and grass and moss which cover the surface of the natural world.

Olive is the colour of the new leaf unfolding; it is the colour of the forest; the colour of the evergreen, the pine. It is the colour of chlorophyll, of nature, of the plant: the creation of the leaf through light and the interactiveness of the sun. This is a powerful chemical process; it is the process of the life force coming to earth and offering its vitality through the plant. Olive Green is an energy which is powerfully regenerating on many levels.

This part of the heart centre, the lower part, is that which connects us with our surroundings, through the lower half of the body. 'Our feet are our understanding.' Those people who have suffered emotional disconnection or connection with pain in their lives can use this colour to regenerate that emotional field, to restore faith and trust and confidence. The Olive is the part of the heart centre which connects us with the physical world into which we have incarnated, helping us to link our consciousness with the world which feeds and sustains us. It can be used to reconnect us with our earthly environment, even opening our minds to the planes of the realms of the devas, the spirit beings traditionally portrayed as fairies and elves who take care of plants and minerals.

The Olive fruit in its natural state has a bitter taste: it has to undergo a chemical process whereby the bitterness is withdrawn before it becomes edible and nutritious. So it can be seen as a metaphor for the spiritual process. Olive has the capacity for helping us to withdraw pain and bitterness which has been stored within the heart.

It is a colour which helps us to find emotional strength and stamina. The Olive tree grows on stony ground, in climates which are hot and dry. It has to dig its roots deep into the soil in order to find the nourishment it needs. So the colour Olive can support us in times of difficulty when we need to find endurance and strength. Such stamina is also offered to us in seaweed, often of an Olive Green colour, which is rich in the minerals that strengthen our physical frame. The Olive colour can help us to find great perseverance on many levels: physical and emotional as well as mental and spiritual.

The Olive also offers us the promise of new land, of gentler times ahead. The dove flew out from Noah's Ark after the devastation of the flood and brought back an olive branch as a sign that new life was springing forth. Olive oil, too, was used in candles as a source of light for thousands of years. Olive trees are planted ahead for the future: a sign of permanence and trust. Olive oil is used by priests in the last rites before a person dies, helping to provide a bridge between this world and the next dimension.

The Olive branch is also a traditional symbol for peace. Where there has been conflict and there is a wish to resolve it, we offer the Olive branch, letting go of bitterness and bringing wisdom into our communication.

The Olive used in the uniforms of soldiers signifies something more than just the camouflage which protects those who wear it from harm. It has also to do with power. In a large sense, the use of such a colour in this connection camouflages the power of hidden weapons in an age where armed conflict often happens at long distance. And Olive has also to do with authority and leadership. Part of this is our own power and leadership quality as individuals.

Could it be that as we resolve the difficulties associated with the three lower energy centres we may begin to find our true power? Olive Green is a colour which we connect in *Aura-Soma* particularly with the quality of feminine leadership: the leadership which comes from the wisdom of the heart. Olive can be used to strengthen our resonance, confidence in ourselves; our willingness and desire, our ability and talent to lead others. This energy can be dangerous if used in a negative connotation – power can always be mis-used – but it can be very positive if applied in the right way. This is part of each person's individual responsibility. I noticed when working the Olive over Olive bottle that for a while I became very bossy towards some of my colleagues... The Olive energy can motivate the hearts and feelings of others in need of leadership and in need of upliftment.

Both the solar plexus and the heart chakra reside at the centre of the body. Olive Green is the bridge between them: it brings together the higher and the lower aspects of ourselves; it links the permanent and the impermanent. It enables us to balance the love of ourselves with the love of others; it helps us to balance the intellect with the emotions, enabling us to think with the heart.

Thus Olive can help us to work positively with our emotions. To identify with the emotions is to allow ourselves to be bound to them and ruled by them, so that we follow them all the way. Olive helps us to release those identifications, enabling us to laugh at ourselves. It can bring the joy of the Yellow energy into the emotional body, which is part of the great regenerative power of this energy.

Imbalance of this chakra may lead to a state of dissatisfaction and discontent; sometimes even the feeling of persecution. The Olive wood is exceptionally hard: a person very drawn towards Olive may find it difficult to bend, displaying inflexibility in their feeling and thinking. Such a state of mind and heart is likely to repercuss on the physical, producing a resistance to movement which manifests, for example, in the joints, making us as stubborn and motionless as a mule. When we get stuck into our ideas, how well do we dance, or climb over a gate?

This characteristic of resistance seems to have been reflected in the response of many people to the very colour Olive itself. It is a very powerful colour, and it seems to carry within it a deep challenge. There are many who have been repelled by Olive on first meeting it; and this response is often replaced later by one of enormous enthusiasm, once the initial opposition to the vibration is overcome.

Olive can also bring the clarity of the Yellow energy into the heart, enabling us to see clearly our own path, helping us to find a true sense of direction. Thus, when the fear of movement is surmounted, the Olive energy enables us to move forward with confidence and ease, venturing out to meet the world. We can go with the flow, moving with the ever-changing, ever-scintillating dance of creation.

Olive is cleansing and disinfectant; and it is also calming. Pine has long been used in cleaning solutions as a freshener, and as an ingredient for soothing bath lotions. It is a colour which may be used in many contexts to soothe and calm. It is useful on scalds or burns, where the skin has been damaged by an excess of light. This is the Green which rebinds us, and soothes energy which has reached a chaotic level and needs to be redressed and reassembled.

Olive is the Green of nature, and an aspect of the heart. It is the balance for the heart centre and it can be used in many different situations to heal and soothe, to reboost and regenerate; to regain awareness where awareness has been lost. This colour is the colour of the earth mother, the connection with the natural world. It is a colour which connects us with ancient times and which is just resurfacing to be used again.

GREEN

Green is the very centre, the heart centre. It is the fourth chakra out of the traditional seven: there are three above it and three below. It is where the Blue from above, which represents the Divine Will, comes together in equal balance with the Yellow of the individual will from below. Man, standing upright in the world, all chakras open to receive the universal life force, can be seen as being poised between two triangles of energy: one comes down from above; the other moves upwards from below (*see* Plate 16).

The resolution of those two energies, the heavenly and the earthly, is contained within the Green of the open heart. It offers us the possibility that the little will of our ego, our drive and ambition, may align itself with the greater Will, once the heart chakra is awakened. Then will we find harmony and space and direction and truth. True self-realization is the discovery of self in relation to divinity.

Green is the heart, and the reflection of our heart in nature. It provides sustenance and growth, life, and balance. It is the colour of love freely given, the expression of our hearts. It is the communication of our thoughts, our feelings and our deeds.

Green represents the world. It represents a shared space. It is that space in which each may participate, offering the gift of the unique quality and talent which is their individual self. It represents for mankind the possibility of a quantum leap in consciousness, where we may move beyond the major concerns of the first three chakras – survival, dependency, and the difficulties of power and the ego – and into a new state of awareness. While the heart chakra remains unawakened the tendency will be to focus merely upon our emotional needs; when the light is brought to bear upon it we may find that the heart is the vehicle of truth. The awakening of the heart chakra offers the possibility for us to awaken to ourselves and each other in a new way: to find that we can communicate, person to person, group to group, nation to nation, through an open heart from a point of inner truth. Here is a key issue, at the dawning of a new epoch, as we attempt to integrate the lessons of the past.

Man has a place which is unique within the animal kingdom. Animals, by their place in the evolution of consciousness, are focused on their need for food and warmth and shelter; and on pleasure. The gift of human life is the invitation to progress beyond this towards a greater awareness. This process begins in the Yellow, with the development of the individual will and the discovery of self. The opportunity within the Green, in moving beyond the desires of the individual will, is to expand our humanity.

The opening of the heart chakra has other implications. If we have overcome the basic fears around our survival, conquered our need for dependency and co-dependency and discovered our individual strength, we may come to a new understanding: this is the realization that we looked at in the 'Cosmic Connections' chapter: that the whole of the universe is interconnected and thus interdependent. What affects one being also affects all other beings. Such interdependency is very different from emotional dependency: it is the realization, for example, that our own lives are intimately linked to the life of the trees which provide us with the oxygen which sustains us. Our very breathing depends upon air which is shared; and each new breath creates an opportunity for expansion, as we open the lungs and the heart. Green is the acknowledgement of our need for the sea, for water, for the air which we breathe and the creatures and plants which nourish us; for the body of the earth itself. It is our recognition of our responsibility to care for all of these as they care for us. The sharing is universal, cosmic.

When the heart chakra begins to awaken we can begin really to *feel* the interconnectedness of the universe. We can recognize the reality of the living, moving energies which comprise our universe, and to understand that in relating to one another we are involved in the constant exchange of energy. If we are focused on our needs then the likelihood is that much of that energy will have some negative connotations. With the Green comes the beginning of trust, so that we come to relationship not from a place of fear when we will tend unconsciously to draw on the resources of those around us, but instead ready to share with others from inner resources which are rich and full.

'There is a Green hill far away... beyond the City wall.' The words of the hymn refer to Calvary and the crucifixion of Christ: the ultimate opening of the heart chakra to encompass the whole of humanity; the sacrifice of self.

In the grounds of Dev Aura, the *Aura-Soma* teaching centre which Vicky Wall created in Tetford, there is a memorial garden which was created for her two years after her death. Beside the gate which leads to this garden is a small plaque on which is written the biblical phrase which she quoted more often than any other: 'I cast mine mine eyes to the hills from whence cometh my help.'

Green is truth, balance, direction and space. It is harmony and harmonizers: those working quietly behind the scenes to ensure the smooth running of the whole. It is faith, hope, acceptance and trust. It is nature and the love of nature. It is symbolized by the Green Man, the traditional God of nature. Green symbolizes the ideals of those committed to ecological activity: Greenpeace and the Green political parties spreading rapidly around the planet. It is open spaces and Green trees. It is the colour of leaves in summer: wide open and fully formed. A tree is well rooted in the earth, and reaches up to the sky above. It is a symbol of growth and the stretching of oneself upwards towards the light. Even in its rootedness to the earth, it shows independence by its upright strength and firmness, and freedom of spirit by the rising of its sap. A tree looks in all directions at once: North, South, West and East; above and below. It represents balance and poise; the ability to see all sides of a question, to exercise discrimination. Green can help us towards such tree-like panoramic awareness, enabling us to make decisions from the heart: where to be, what to do, and when to do it.

Trees have a connection with time as well as space: the passing of each year of their life produces a ring in their slowly expanding trunk. The oak is an example of a tree which spans the lifetimes of many human generations, connecting us with the past and the future. The planet Saturn is also associated with Green, and is the planet known as Cronos, or Old Father Time.

What a lot trees have to teach us, and to offer. Many trees are now recognized for their healing power: oaks are one of the strongest and most positive. Vicky Wall often recommended people to hug trees, and named the Green/Green bottle the 'Go Hug a Tree' bottle.

The association of Green with nature gives it a quality of peaceful calm, as well as space. The walls of institutions such as hospitals and prisons are often painted Green. While this may induce peace and calm acceptance in those housed therein, it also creates the illusion of space when in reality many such institutions deprive their patients and inmates of the opportunity for personal space and the right to decision making.

The selection of Green, therefore, may indicate not only that the person has a love of nature and truth, but also that there is a search for direction and a need for space. Such a choice may show that a person finds it hard to claim their own space. They may be over-generous in letting others into their space. The unfulfilled need for space may then manifest as an expansion on the physical level, either as a gain in weight, or more particularly in the formation of tumours. It may express itself as a problem in the lungs: a difficulty in finding sufficient breath.

A person who is unable to ask for the space which they need may suffer from difficulties around the sense of their own worth, which leads them to value another person's space above their own. This might then manifest as jealousy or envy. This is a quality which, while uncomfortable, can make one acutely sensitive and observant about other people. The gift in this is to apply that same observation to oneself, enabling one to see the truth of his own nature. The truly Green person is a genuine seeker after the truth, even when what is revealed is not what the ego might have hoped for. Where Green appears as a challenge, maybe there is a difficulty around the question of truth: doubt, or perhaps deception.

Green offers us a new direction and a new place. It may greet us at a crossroads, showing us a signpost. It is the Green light, the signal to go; or the American Green Card, which opens the way for us to explore new territory. Thus it helps us to let go of old identifications, old habits. It enables us to let go of the deepest and most ancient emotional patterns: those karmic patterns which draw into our lives over and over again the same relationships and the same difficulties. Karma is the Eastern term for the law of cause and effect. Another way of expressing this is that we reap whatever we sow; or it could be understood as the spiritual equivalent of a law in physics: that for every action there is an equal and opposite reaction. To overcome our negative karma we need to understand the cause, in order to experience different effects.

The full opening of the heart chakra enables us to overcome our need for emotional food, to mend the broken heart (which may be crying out in the pain of angina) and to resolve our feelings of jealousy and envy. Once the jealousy is understood there is no more need to identify with its emotion, which leads to another gift within the Green energy: freedom. The Green of the earth offers enough space for everyone. Like Red, the Green offers the opportunity to connect with the earth, which offers limitless expanse and freedom.

We know that Green, when used in art, contains Yellow and Blue in equal parts. Thus the challenge aspect of the Green must still include a degree of fear: the hidden Yellow within the Green. As the Yellow is hidden, so the fears within this vibration tend to be hidden and irrational, and they apply particularly to the issue of space: claustrophobia, agoraphobia. There may be a fear of being seen; an uncertainty around one's own identity which produces the need to hide: a concealing of one's own truth, or the hiding of one's light under a bushel.

Green is the colour of the heart; therefore it has a close connection with the Pink energy of love and compassion. Green offers a space and a route whereby the loving quality of the Pink may find expression. Love must find an outlet, and this outlet is the heart. Green may thus be understood as active compassion; love expressed rather than contained.

Blackfriar's Bridge in London, which was Black for many years, was long known as a suicide spot. When it was painted

Green, the suicide rate made a dramatic drop to a third of the previous numbers. Here is astonishing testimony to the soothing effect of the Green energy. How sad that it was subsequently painted Black once again.

Green is a blanket colour, soothing and calming, like the soft leaves quietly littered over the floor of the forest. It is peace and the wide open spaces of grass and trees. It is expansion. It is the link with the physical world, joining us with the power of nature. Green provides nourishment for the body, the spirit and the heart.

Camilla

Bottle No. 21: Green/Pink, known as New Beginning for Love, is a bottle that, when indicated as a gift, shows a strong, mature person. Their male and female aspects are well balanced; they have a clear sense of direction and a clarity about and loyalty towards whatever it is they have committed themselves to in the world. They offer love unconditionally and receive it easily. As a challenge, this bottle often indicates a difficulty in giving and receiving love, and a need to find not only love but also direction and space.

Camilla came as a student on a workshop shortly after her husband had left her for a new partner. She was a little brittle at first. Her face was set and she was rather more demanding than many students during the first few days of the course. She expressed dissatisfaction over the food and the temperature of the showers in the very modestly priced hotel in which the course was being held.

Halfway through the week she requested a private consultation. The tears flowed fast almost the second that the first observations about her colours were made. There was a leaning towards Green in the selection; most notably Green/Pink in second place.

It emerged that Camilla, though angry and hurt, was also

quite relieved at the break-up of the marriage. There had long been power struggles between her and her husband, both of them seeking dominance in the relationship. Camilla was aware of a pattern of jealousy and possessiveness which had characterized her earlier relationships. She began to see that one of the many unconscious decisions she had made in marrying Denis was to choose someone whom she would not be able to control; though she had not long been in the relationship before the usual pattern had asserted itself and she had tried to control him. The inevitable battles had soon begun.

Camilla had known that she had become set in a pattern of putting on a good face not only socially but even with her family, who had clear ideas regarding the indissolubility of marriage. So for several years she had been feeling bored with the self-deception and the deception of others. She was also aware that there were plenty of things she would like to do with her life, but none of them seemed compatible with her relationship. Denis was a lawyer from a wealthy and conservative background. Camilla's interests were leading her towards yoga and meditation and the reading of increasingly 'way out' literature. She wanted to take a counselling course. Denis scoffed at all of these. Camilla liked to keep up to date with all the latest rock groups. Denis liked to go to the Promenade Concerts and listen to Beethoven's *Ninth Symphony*.

Thus, in her head, Camilla was well aware of the service Denis had done her in leaving her. She nevertheless experienced sharp pangs of resentment, and of jealousy towards the new woman in his life – particularly as she was alone.

Camilla knew that this relationship had stifled her potential, and that she wanted a wider place in the world. She saw that the pattern of jealousy and control in the past had been based on fear and self-doubt, and that she was mentally and physically strong. She saw, too, that she had gifts of intuition and empathy and unlimited funds of unconditional love – and humour – once she could open her heart to receive love and communication from those around her. The Green indicated a strong heart quality, as well as a deep feeling of connection with the natural world. The Pink, we often say to people, can only be expressed through the Green; in other words, through the heart. Here, then, was the ideal combination for Camilla to find a way through what had previously been an impasse, and find a new way for herself in the world – and a new beginning for the giving and the receiving of love.

Camilla relaxed considerably during the week, laughing much more often then she cried. A few months later she left to go abroad, with her new lover. That was the last I heard...

TURQUOISE

As the journey continues upwards from the Green area of the heart, and towards the Blue of the throat, we meet something in between the two: this is the colour Turquoise, which still contains something of the Green energy. It is as if the pure Emerald Green, the heart within the heart which exists at the core of the being containing the very essence of our individual truth, has a layer of protection below it and above. This protection forms also a route whereby we may find access to this inner truth. Just below the pure Green is the Olive Green, connecting the Yellow of the individual will to the heart, bridging the thinking and the feeling, the individual and the universal, and providing a context within which the individual will may be creatively expressed in the world. Within the Olive Green the Yellow energy is still dominant: it has a greater proportion of Yellow than Blue. The pure Green contains equal parts of Yellow and Blue. Above the pure Green is the Turquoise: a Bluer shade of Green. This colour contains a greater proportion of Blue than Yellow: it is where the heart moves towards the Blue of the throat in order to communicate its message. Where the Yellow signifies the little, individual, will, Blue stands for the Heaven energy: Thy Will, or the greater Will. This is where the individual may overcome the needs of the ego and submit to the wider plan; thus the heart may transcend itself and find expression.

Turquoise enables us to find the creative communication of the heart through the feeling side of the being. It has to do more with feeling and intuition than with rational thought. Turquoise is the colour of emotion, of feeling, expressed through word, through silence, through thought, through all forms of communication. It is the communication not of one to one, but from one to the many. Turquoise brings the Blue of communication into the Green of the world. Thus it has an association with teaching; with the feeling behind the words which are spoken.

I should like to see a time when *Aura-Soma* becomes a standard part of teacher training, with refresher courses especially created for headmasters. Education has for so long focused on the intellect. We need to educate the emotions, so that we understand what the inner child is attempting to say when we project the pain of that wounded child on to those children in our care. Similarly, how wonderful it would be if we could gain something of that understanding before becoming parents.

The communication connected with Turquoise is wide, and deep as the ocean. It may be the written word in letter or poetry; it may be artistic creation, be it sculpture, painting, dance, drama. It may be movement, singing or chanting. All these activities are surrounded by the colour Turquoise.

Turquoise is a natural progression from the colour Pink. At first we will feel; but these feelings are more valuable if they can be communicated and shared with others so they can be understood, remedied, healed; so they can spread their teaching. If this is to be, the Pink must find the Blue, must transform into Turquoise, must be spoken and communicated. The Pink can only find expression through the heart: through the Green or the Turquoise. There is a *Balance* combination of Pink over Turquoise: its name is the Birth of Venus. It is the acknowledgement of what may happen when the Pink energy finds its way through to the communication of the heart.

The colour Turquoise is associated with the ancient civilizations, particularly Atlantis and Lemuria – these were two of the very earliest civilizations, perhaps better described as experiments with life on earth, which both perished through the abuse of power – and it is also found frequently among the ethnic cultures, in their pottery and in sand paintings. It is found, along with Gold leaf and other rich and exotic colours, on the walls of Eastern shrines. The gemstone Turquoise was recognized in Egyptian times, and more recently in the Native American cultures, as a powerfully healing stone.

Turquoise, along with Magenta, is referred to as one of the New Age rays: it is a colour associated with Aquarius, the water bearer; the astrological sign of the New Aeon. Water is the element which is associated with feeling, with the emotions. The association of Turquoise with this new time is partly because it is a colour which only came recently to man's consciousness; but more than this, the Turquoise represents a newly-awakening chakra just above and to the right of the heart. Many psychics report on this new energy field appearing in man's aura at this time. From an *Aura-Soma* point of view this is seen as a general increase of energy moving into this area as more and more people awaken to the heart aspect of their consciousness. This was first acknowledged in recent times by an Indian visionary and saint named Ramana Maharshi. His belief was that mankind's route to enlightenment could be sought through exploring and answering one question: 'Who am I?' The answer to this would provide the key to our illumination, enabling each individual to take responsibility for themselves – an essential prerequisite to the survival of mankind and of the planet.

Ramana Maharshi gave the newly awakening chakra a name: Ananda Khanda, which means the abode of bliss. Bliss is the possibility of what we may offer to ourselves when the answer has been found to the question 'Who am I?', and when we have accepted responsibility for what it is that we are. The answer lies in moving the Ananda Khanda from the right side to the centre of the chest, thus fully awakening the Turquoise energy and the true creative communication from the feeling side of ourselves. Thus it is the colour of the inner teacher within ourselves.

It is also, therefore, a colour which may indicate self-reliance and a free-thinking independence. Such independence, based as it is on the connection with the feelings and the responsibility of the heart, is likely to accompany a humanitarian consciousness rather than a tendency towards isolation. Where idealism is misplaced, the Turquoise can indicate delusion: the possibility of fooling ourselves through seeing things the way we should like them to be rather than as they are.

Turquoise is a colour which we associate with the sea. Through the sea it connects us with the deep, collective unconscious of mankind: with the long-lost civilizations of the deep past, such as Atlantis. The knowledge and teaching which they contained is written into the unconscious memory of man rather than into the history books. Turquoise therefore carries with it the possibility of a new kind of individuation: the individuation which may happen when we make the connection with the deeper, feeling, unconscious aspect of ourselves. Carl Jung found that as his patients moved towards greater wholeness, mandala-like images began to appear in their dreams: these are symbols from the collective unconscious emerging and becoming integrated at a conscious level.

The most powerful symbol of the Turquoise energy lives in

the sea: the dolphin. Dolphins can communicate with each other over very long distances. Their communication is wide, telepathic, and very much based in the feeling. They have many more neural connections within their brains than we do; but they invest their abundant mental and emotional energy in ways to play rather than in ways to work. Knowing there are plenty of fish in the sea, they feel no need to focus on survival as we do; so they cultivate a playful spirit. They are spontaneous. They also focus on caring for the young, the old, and the helpless, co-operating to care for any of their members who are sick or in need.

Another consequence of discovering and communicating who we are, and taking responsibility for that, is that we may find freedom. This has also to do with the overcoming of survival issues and becoming creative and playful. Dolphins are creatures who have found freedom in the sea. Swimming-pools, too, symbolize for us the possibility of freedom, movement, and play, within the element of water.

Turquoise has a transdimensional quality. Not only does it connect us with the oceanic universal consciousness symbolized by the sea, enabling us to move from the conscious dimension into the unconscious one: it is also the colour of the connection with other realms such as those of the angels and the devas, and with beings from outer space. This is similar to the dolphin consciousness touched on above: if a dolphin is in distress then all others of the same school will know about it across oceans.

On another level, Turquoise is intimately connected with the communication network which has been brought about through the development of silicon chip technology. At this time of entering a new phase of our history, the Aquarian Age, we are able to make instant communication with any other part of the globe. Part of the downfall of previous civilizations such as Atlantis and Lemuria was caused by misuse of this same energy: the manipulation of technology through such things as genetic engineering, where man played God and abused power and knowledge.

This is all part of the Turquoise package. Silica and the microchip have enabled us to deliver the same message to millions of people all over the world at the same time. The challenge is to learn the lessons of the past in order to prevent another downfall; to take responsibility for the quality of that communication. The network of satellites may be used to manipulate; or it may be used to educate and create, raising the planetary vibrations for a quantum leap in awareness. The Turquoise energy signifies a profound change in our relationship with time and space: both in terms of travel and communication our planet has shrunk, as we have moved from a carbon cycle to a silicon one.

Turquoise therefore carries within it a reminder that everything is interconnected. We need to take responsibility for the quality of our thoughts as well as of our conscious communication. Communication is what we receive as well as what we project. So if we were all to stop giving energy to gossip and bad news then it would have nothing to feed on.

Responsibility, loving communication, freedom, a warm Turquoise sea: all these suggest the possibility of deep peace and tranquillity. The presence of Turquoise might, of course, indicate the reverse: the deep need for serenity and calm; a profound sense that the opportunity for loving communication is absent. It may also hint at the calm which precedes a storm. Turquoise has a calming effect; and it may be used to ease those people who find it difficult to air their heart.

So the essential word in relation to Turquoise is communication. It is the integration of the Green of the heart and the Blue of the throat. The throat and heart working in harmony together brings about great healing of the voice through counselling, meditation, chanting and singing. Also it opens up the aspects of powerful intuition, empathy, clairaudience and clairsentience, the ability to hear and feel beyond the normal senses of mankind. The psychic must be grounded in the heart: then the clear seeing and feeling begins.

Paul

The strength in Bottle No. 43: Turquoise/Turquoise, called Creativity, is the ability to communicate creatively, and widely, from the heart; the communication is often through means beyond the verbal, such as art or music or dance. It indicates someone who is self-reliant and able to use the experience of their life to connect deeply with their own inner teacher. It can be a bottle of great inspiration. In common with all the other bottles, and all the other colours, this bottle will sometimes show aspects of the personality which present difficulties. So, particularly in the second position, this *Balance* combination tends to indicate that the person is unwilling to connect with the deeper, less conscious, aspects of himself. He (or she) may be very much out of touch with their feelings; and being thus at a distance from himself he experiences deep feelings of rejection and separation from others.

Paul was a successfully self-employed businessman who was clearly used to running his own show. Quick-witted and jovial, he joked his way through 25 minutes of the session. Since all the bottles were block colours, i.e. the same colour top and bottom, it became rapidly clear that here was someone whose habit of avoiding looking further than skin deep at his own life was pretty thoroughly established. The impression was of a talented person endowed with wide-ranging gifts; yet somehow scattered. It was as though the different parts of himself existed separately and out of harmony with one another. He could not, literally, 'get it together'. After nearly half an hour the jokes began to subside and I asked Paul what he had hoped for in coming for an *Aura-Soma* session. He paused, before replying quietly that he had suffered several bouts of severe depression in the previous few years which had rendered him incapable for weeks at a time of running his business. He admitted that these difficult periods were repercussing heavily on his family life. At the very end of this first session Paul remarked rather suddenly that he had been adopted at the age of six weeks by a married couple who were kind and gentle and who had given him, in his own words, 'everything that anyone could ask for'.

Paul left, taking with him the Turquoise/Turquoise bottle, with instructions to shake it and use it twice a day for the next three or four weeks. It would not have surprised me if he had not returned. I felt uncertain that he had heard much of what the bottles had revealed, particularly as the lack of movement and flow between all these block colours had made interpretation something of a challenge.

He did return, however, over a year later. This was a very different experience from the first session. Paul had embarked on a search, which had several strands. First, he had decided to discover who his original parents had been, and had eventually found that his father had been a teacher of classical literature and his mother one of his students. This knowledge had helped Paul to understand why he had always felt unfulfilled by the world of small business in which he had grown up, and perpetuated in his own adult life. He had long yearned vaguely for something, but not knowing what it was he sought he had continued in his quest for material achievement. He knew now that he was seeking a sense of purpose, and he had begun writing in his spare time. He still had no idea how he wished to spend his life, but the writing was taking on a life of its own and Paul was surprised by the ideas which seemed to be expressing themselves through him. He had suffered several more periods of depression, but he was less frightened by the sense of being out of control, instead accepting these times as fuel for what it was that he wished to write.

The most significant change in Paul, it appeared, was the movement towards seeking his own truth. He had recognized that, in common with so many others who had been adopted, he had made a habit, since early childhood, of lying. It was this habit which had kept him for so many years from his own truth, so that he had simply not known what belonged to him and what belonged to others. The game had become the apparent reality which obscured the true goal. It was with some fervour that he now applied himself to the search.

For Paul the experience of the Turquoise energy was only the beginning of a process which was to go much further. Each stage that is worked through, or in other words each therapeutic bottle, may be seen as the overcoming of another obstacle on the assault course of a life. Every stage, when welcomed as a challenge which we have built into the set-up, becomes an opportunity not only to build up strength and develop our gifts, but also to remove a layer of conditioning which has clouded our perception of the truth.

BLUE

The fifth main chakra covers the area of the throat. It is the area of the Blue, the first of the three primary colours. The Blue is the colour of the sky – out of which appeared first the sun and then the earth. It is thus closely linked to the primary source of creation: Blue is the colour which we associate with Heaven.

The colour Blue connects us with the 'Divine Blueprint'. Things are not random; there is a Divine plan, and each of us is part of that plan. Our own Divine Blueprint could be described as the plan, or the map, which, in co-operation with those in the spiritual realms, we drew up before coming into incarnation. Being human we keep losing the map.

Blue is a colour which gives great protection: the earth is surrounded by a film of blue which protects its surface from being fried by the harmful wavelengths from the sun. The colour Blue may offer us protection in a way similar to the protection of the earth by the Blue sky. Blue is approaching the cooler and calmer end of the spectrum: where Red is stimulating, Blue is pacifying. It is a healing and retardant colour. It is a colour which prevents progression, slowing things down and offering us the opportunity to be still. It is a

colour which discourages disease and disharmony, and all
negative vibrations.

The throat is the area of the body through which we receive
the primary source of our sustenance: the breath of life, which
is constantly available to us from the air around us and the Blue
sky above. The in-breath may thus be seen as carrying the
voice of God, the source, or whichever word we choose to
convey the energy behind creation: 'In the beginning was the
Word'. The out-breath then passes over the vocal chords to
carry our own voice. Blue is thus not only the colour of speech
but also the colour of listening. It is the colour of hearing; and
knowing. Blue, therefore, is the central colour in
communication. Below it is the Turquoise, which denotes the
'feeling' communication emanating from the depths of the
being; above it is the Royal Blue which is to do with the
communication of something which is fed in from above:
those things which we receive and have the power to censor
before we give them out. Blue, as in skies and sapphires, is the
straight communication which comes through us as though
through an open door. It is the communication of what we
think.

Blue is therefore communication both on an earthly level,
the communication from one to another of the thoughts; and
also on the higher level. It is the bridge across to spiritual
dimensions: the Blue doorway to psychic realms; the trance
medium or the channel who brings through the
communication from other spheres. It is the colour of Akasha.
This is the name given to the fifth element, the all-pervading
space within which all the remaining four elements exist and
interact. Those psychics who have highly developed powers of
communication beyond the level of normal human
communication are able to connect with the 'Akashic records',
which could be described as a cosmic library in which is
contained information about the past, the present and the

future. Hence the prophecies of rare men such as Edgar Cayce, as well as the insights about the deep past which empowered him to bring about thousands of miracle cures in extreme and often otherwise incurable cases. Inspiration sometimes comes to all of us 'out of the Blue': something communicated to us from the Blue which surrounds us all.

Blue is the place for change: from one dimension to another in terms of communication, or in the processes of birth and death, where it offers the possibility of peaceful transition. 'Be still and know that I am God.'

The illumination and awakening of the Blue chakra, therefore, has to do with communication, and relationship. The issues or the difficulties in the Blue are around relating: the whole of the way we express ourselves in relation to our thinking. It is the way in which we process our thoughts and make them available both to ourselves and to others; our relationship with our own mental processes. Thus the awakening of this centre carries the possibility of deep mental peace, turning off the jumble of thoughts which normally move ceaselessly through our minds, and making the conscious surrender of the will to the Greater Will. This, once accepted, will bring us the deepest possible peace: 'the peace that passeth all understanding'. It is unlikely that this chakra is in a fully awakened state in many beings currently on this planet. Really from this point on the journey of evolution we are looking at the potential for the future rather than the reality as experienced by more than a few highly conscious beings. One step at a time, however; on the journey each of the chakras may awaken from time to time, for a while.

Blue is the calm tranquillity and serenity of a cloudless summer sky or of a blue lagoon. It is the colour of Forget-Me-Nots. It is the Blue bird of happiness. It is the colour of Laramar, a rare crystal of a beautiful pale Blue, whose function is to help us to connect with a divine quality of love; to rise above our human limitations and find an unconditional resource of love even when there is great conflict. It is the colour of Mary the Madonna; or Kwan Yin, the Chinese Goddess of Compassion; and of the divine Hindu beings Krishna and Vishna. In Buddhic philosophy, Blue is the colour of pure mind: the clear mind uncluttered by thought. Whatever arises within the mind, the thoughts and emotions, behind it is the Blue sky; just as the Blue sky is always behind any clouds which may arise to obscure our perception of its clarity. Blue is, therefore, the colour of divinity, communication and the deepest possible peace. Yet, as with all the colours, there is duality contained here. The caution is, 'What price peace?' Too much Blue may indicate that a person will choose peace at any price: anything for a quiet life. Where not saying what we feel is a Turquoise issue, not saying what we think is a Blue one. The consequence of such 'peace at any price' is the absence of any real peace at all.

Blue is the colour of high ideals and principles. It can indicate, within one drawn towards this hue, qualities of great patience. It can show that skills have been developed in communication not only on the outer level, but within oneself; so that the right brain has become active, releasing the intuitive and feminine creative aspect of the being. Where there is deep peace the creative energy can flow.

Blue, the primary primary, is the predominant colour within the light which reaches the earth. It is the energy which reaches down towards the earth from above. So it is clearly the colour which is closest to divinity. Vicky Wall cautioned us, however, against being 'so heavenly we are no earthly use'. The selection of a lot of Blue may indicate the desire to be in Heaven, or perhaps the desire not to enter into earthly existence, and the Blue can be an avoidance of coming into contact with one's responsibilities on the earth plane.

One of the key characteristics of the Blue, and another

aspect of the journey, is independence: this is the polar opposite of the Orange energy, which carries the challenge of dependency and co-dependency. In one way the Blue is the solution to the Orange dilemma: within the Blue is the possibility of finding a deep peace within ourselves, that we may be able to come to terms with the issues to do with patterns of addiction, of dependency and co-dependency and to move towards our own independence.

Yet in another way the need for Blue may indicate someone who keeps themselves separate because of a desire to escape. The challenge is to find the true independence which then enables us to live in a balanced state of interdependence. This is the possibility already touched on in the Green: when independence has been fully realized, we can enter fully into interdependence. This is the living out of the recognition of our need for co-operation at all levels. The key to this is the finding of peace, which is perhaps the quintessential feature of the Blue energy. The *Balance* bottle number 2 is Blue over Blue: its name is the Peace bottle. Not only, as noted many times already in these pages, are we the colours we choose: those colours also reflect what it is that we need. The selection of Blue may well indicate a deep need for peace.

While Blue denotes the divine mother, the Goddess, the universal mother energy, it also contains the male element. There is a strong association in the Blue with the masculine, both in the earthly and the spiritual sense. Blue often indicates issues around authority: difficulties with the father and consequently with the male identity within oneself; both on an earthly level and on the more abstract level of accepting what is described as the Divine Blueprint. There has to be a depth of peace before we can truly say 'I will that Thy Will be done through me'.

Such rejection of authority is reflected in some of the symbolism around the colour Blue. The 1960s brought a rebellion among the youth culture against the structure and social mores of the day. A dominant symbol of this rebellion was the wearing of Blue jeans: these at once signified the rejection of the status quo and the desire to be part of a social group. This duality is echoed in the Blue uniforms worn by the services: the Navy and the Airforce, for example. Such uniforms indicate a tendency towards being an individual as well as the wish to be interdependent, part of a group or subculture. There are many other Blue uniforms: they may contain something of this duality, but above all they denote the idea of service. 'Thy Will be done' is a Blue statement, or intention, which often grounds itself in occupations which serve: nurses worldwide, for example, wear Blue; so do the dustmen in Paris and the street cleaners in Tokyo.

Blue is the colour which has long been associated with conservatism in general, and specifically with the Conservative party in British politics. This, again, has partly to do with the social grouping aspect of the Blue energy; but also with another feature of Blue, which is a tendency to need to hold on, resisting change, and to find difficulty in letting go. It can indicate too much acquisitiveness, which leads to stagnation. We hold on to something; it gets stuck in the throat. The person choosing a lot of Blue will probably have more difficulty in clearing out their back room to provide fodder for the local jumble sale, or perhaps in losing weight, than the person drawn to Red or Orange.

The authority within Blue manifests in numerous ways. Apart from conservatism, and Blue uniforms, it is also the colour of diplomacy and refinement: noble ancestry is denoted by Blue blood, and cultural elitism and academic excellence are indicated by the term Bluestocking.

The possibility of independence within the Blue is a gift and a strength. It is the possibility of experiencing a sense of aloneness in the most positive sense: the sense of all-one-ness rather than of isolation and loneliness. Before this sense is achieved, the presence of Blue frequently indicates such a state of loneliness; of separation rather than cohesion. The term Blue movies refers to an experience of sexuality which essentially is at one remove. It is voyeurism rather than involvement. We often, too, use the phrase 'feeling Blue' to indicate periods of despondency. Blue may indicate frigidity with its consequent sense of isolation. It may suggest introversion and sadness.

Blue is not only the calming end of the spectrum but also the cooling one. It cools not only the fires of the heart but the fires of the body. It quenches the fires of passion and anger. It may be used in situations where we are out of control and chaos reigns, pouring oil on troubled waters and helping us to reflect on our surroundings. The Archangel Michael is often portrayed in Blue, with a sword of insight which slays the dragon, which is the symbol of the difficulties within our lower nature: the problems of passion and desire and so on. The sword is not one which destroys these 'dragons'; rather it provides the insight which enables us to understand them. Rather than becoming caught up in pleasure at the expense of happiness, which is a possibility within the Orange and the lower chakras, we may, with the Blue, find the Blue Bird of Happiness.

Blue enables us to find a sense of trust and faith. It is the colour not of the earthly but of the celestial, universal mother, bringing us the protective, nurturing energy of the Goddess. It is a guiding energy. This is symbolized, in many countries, by the Blue road signs which are associated with the motorways or main roads: we may take many wrong turns and find ourselves in cul-de-sacs; yet in the end it is the acceptance of the Divine Will above the little will which will take us along the main road to our destination.

Bottle No. 3: Blue/Green *The Heart Bottle*

This bottle relates above all to the heart and the emotional aspect of life. It helps those who have difficulty in expressing themselves emotionally, in 'getting things off their chest', so that they may become creative instead of getting heart disease.

A number of us were attending a teachers' course in a hotel which had once been a hospital for patients suffering from tuberculosis. This disease was, among other things, the manifestation on a physical level of a deep holding tendency: the tendency to bottle up, deep in the heart and lungs, emotions such as grief and sorrow. Had *Aura-Soma* been available at the time when this disease was prevalent this bottle could have been a specific for the condition.

Within the first couple of days of the course, not one but two of these Blue/Green bottles exploded spontaneously on their stands. No other bottles did this.

This is a phenomenon now familiar to those acquainted with energy work. Crystals, for example, sometimes behave the same way when the vibration which they hold is urgently needed. There are many situations in which the bottles have acted in this way. For example, on an occasion when I had just finished a sample group 'reading' with some students we returned the bottles to their place on the stand, which happened to be situated just behind the seat of the student whose reading it had been. We had just begun to turn our attention to something else, within a minute or so, when the therapeutic second bottle this student had chosen, and which we had been discussing along with the rest but which had brought especially deep issues, exploded behind her. What a mess ...

We hoped, with the explosion of those Heart bottles in the hotel, that some of the healing energy which they contained would have reached those poor souls who had doubtless died young and painful deaths.

ROYAL BLUE

Royal Blue is the colour of the sky as the day moves towards the night. It is as though the sapphire Blue filter dissolves, becomes transparent, and then we see the stars which in the day are hidden from our senses. The stars, like the moon, were there all the time; but they were obscured from our eyes until the descent of the night. Royal Blue is the colour associated with Nuit, the Egyptian Goddess of the Night, who symbolizes deep wisdom. Royal Blue, therefore, takes us into deep seeing, deep feeling; a new level of understanding.

The Royal Blue brings clarity to the sense organs. During the day we receive sense impressions, then at night in our dreams we still feel, see, and hear things; but those senses are coming from inside and being acted out. Our senses become finer at night-time: it is then that we are likely to connect with the higher mind functions, letting go of the purely physical senses and seeing what is behind the everyday. Where daylight is for normal everyday living, at night there is another part of ourselves which becomes awake.

Royal Blue relates to the sixth energy centre, the brow chakra. This actually contains many of the sensory organs: the eyes, the ears, the nose; and this latter has an intimate relationship with the sense of taste. It relates to the faculties of seeing and hearing, and experiencing. Above that, it is concerned with the refinement of these: with the higher mental faculties of deep seeing, deep hearing and deep feeling. The sixth chakra is the sixth sense. It is connected to the area in the middle of the forehead, the third eye, and to the faculties of clairvoyance, clairaudience and clairsentience. The Royal Blue is the door through to the unconscious. Highly sensitive creatures, particularly those prone to mental disorder, show heightened symptoms at the time of the full moon: this is the time when the fullest light is shone on the unconscious mind.

The caution in the Blue was not to be 'so heavenly that we are no earthly use'. By the time we reach the Royal Blue the Red has reappeared, though in a hidden form: Royal Blue contains two parts Blue to one part Red. With the relationship of the Red energy with the earth, the bringing of a little Red into the Blue symbolizes the beginning of grounding the heavenly energy.

The bridge which links the two hemispheres of the brain is also within the Royal Blue range. Hence its function as an empowering agent for the intuitive, creative aspect of the being. The Royal Blue bridge is also helpful for those making a transition, either towards death or towards life. It helps the memory, both long-term and short-term. At a deeper level, it helps in remembrance, the remembering and the understanding of why we are here.

Royal Blue is associated with Kings and kingliness: with King David, the leader of the Jewish people; with the wisdom of King Solomon. It is a colour associated with the royalty and authority which has its origin in spiritual rather than earthly potency. It is associated with meditation, and with mysticism in its most profound form.

The communication which is a feature of the Royal Blue is of a different kind from the throat chakra communication.

Royal Blue helps us in the deepest communication: the relationship with the entirety of creation, and also with the different aspects of ourselves, linking the various parts like the branches of a tree. It is as though the central observer resides in the Royal area, watching and making connections with the various sub-personalities which appear at different times on the stage of ourselves. The night-time, clear-seeing aspect of the Royal Blue also brings clarity to the sense organs through which we relate, so that within the Royal Blue is the possibility of being creative in the way we relate to ourselves and to others.

In the watching, however, lies also the caution. There is the possibility, within the Royal Blue, of too much detachment. This may result in feelings of arrogance, aloofness, superiority. It could mean extreme loneliness and isolation; more extreme than that of the Blue. It may indicate extreme sobriety: a lack of humour and spontaneity. Sometimes it indicates a state of depression.

Royal Blue brings deep healing through sound, through sight, through all the senses. It is a helpful energy for those who paint and write but who have difficulties with verbal communication.

There is an association between the Royal Blue and the stone Lapis Lazuli. This was the most precious stone in the times of the Egyptian dynasties. Royal Blue is also the energy of Angelite, another precious stone, which is found only in Peru. This stone has a link with the angelic kingdoms. The energies of both these are contained within the Royal Blue *Balance* combinations.

The Royal Blue person loves mystery and the unexpected; he enjoys secrets. As a difficulty this may manifest as a tendency to react to difficulties by isolating himself and withdrawing into a private world; maybe into a world of fantasy. The person heavily drawn towards Royal Blue may be someone who has an extreme tendency to idealize; thus he has difficulty in seeing things as they are. He may be somewhat paranoid or, conversely, a creator of Utopian visions.

There are many similarities between Blue and Royal Blue; but most of the characteristics which already relate to the Blue become more intense and more extreme in the Royal. While, therefore, there is the possibility for profound depression and despondency, and loneliness, there is also the potential for the deepest concentration and clarity. While there may be extreme difficulties with authority, there is also the possibility within the Royal of great creativity within the area of relationship. The Royal Blue person tends to be highly efficient, and capable of enormous determination which means that this is a person who will see things through to their right conclusion. He, or she, has great mental strength and endurance.

What about the journey? If we were to bring about the awakening of the Royal Blue chakra what kinds of things would that imply? The relationship in this sixth chakra is not limited to our relationship with ourselves and with each other. The Royal Blue is also the relationship with everything that exists. Even beyond this, it is also the subject–object relationship of the way in which we put ourselves in relation to what it is that exists. There is the possibility of the whole of our beingness going into the relationship with, for example, a flower: as we look at the flower we may simply see it, or we might experience total empathy with that flower so that we cease to be separate from it and enter into a total relationship with it, which transcends the limitations of subject and object. Again, at this time in our history, such illumination as more than an occasional phenomenon would be likely to occur only infrequently.

Royal Blue offers deep change: deliverance through transmutation. While, to some extent, it may carry the bitterness and the suffering of the Violet, it also has within it the qualities of reconstruction, regeneration and rebirth. It is nurturing and preparatory. It is seen in times of impending transformation: around those preparing to pass into the spiritual world. Royal Blue is the colour of the alchemist: it is seen around those special individuals known as catalysts, who speed the psychical and spiritual development of those they touch. It is lightning and quicksilver. It is more often seen as a fleeting energy than as a constant: it shifts, changes and transforms. It is movement; sudden inspiration. Royal Blue is the highest peak of performance, when performance becomes inspiration.

VIOLET

This is the colour of the seventh and final energy station within the traditional chakra system, and the last one which relates to the physical body. Violet is the crown chakra; our personal connection with the energy of heaven.

The seventh colour is the colour of ritual, magic, mystery and mysticism. Seven of itself is a number of great magic and mystery. We talk of the Seventh Heaven, and the Seven Wonders of the World. The seventh child is often seen to have special gifts. The body of man restores itself every seven years. There are seven chakras, seven bodies from the physical through the subtle, seven notes on a major scale, and seven colours in the rainbow.

Thus Violet represents the end of a cycle. Maybe this has been a long cycle: in the East it is believed that to sleep between Violet sheets promotes longevity of life. A Violet haze may appear above the soil as it is ploughed in preparation for a new cycle of fertility. Violet is the colour of autumn: ripened fruit, and the rotting leaves which nourish the earth for a new season. It is the colour of the final letting go, that something new may be born. Violet is the energy of completion. It is the colour of renewal and regrowth: even the renewal which frees us from karmic injury and bondage, offering karmic absolution.

This colour brings together the Blue and the Red in equal proportions. Thus it represents heaven on earth: spirituality in relation to service. It is the grounding, in the Red, of the divine Blueprint, or of our own higher intentions. It is the colour of attunement and connection with the higher self. It helps us to know what it is that we are here for, what to do and the way to do it. It may indicate the sacrifice of self in the context of peace.

Violet is one of the higher vibrational frequency colours. It has the shortest wavelength of the colours in the visible spectrum of light; and it is the most calming. An obvious example of this is the use in orthodox medicine of ultra-Violet rays, which exist beyond the Violet in the invisible part of the spectrum of light, for calming cancers. Having a short wavelength, it vibrates very fast and is thus very penetrating in its action.

The penetrating nature of Violet gives it a spiritual potency. It is a colour linked with the ability to see into the unknown realms. Violet is spirituality. It is the awareness to look beyond the illusion of reality into the true knowledge of the superconscious. It is the colour of ascension: the transcendence of the physical and the earthly; and the connection with the akashic realms, that space within which all the other elements exist, and upon which is written the history of the universe.

Like Royal Blue, Violet is connected with royalty and authority. Such a connection is symbolized in Japan by the placing of a Violet band around the head of a monarch who is sick. But in general the Violet robe is more likely to be associated with bishops than with kings: a symbol of their representation of Heaven on earth.

Violet is deeply healing. It is, of all colours, the morphine, soothing the pains of body and spirit. The amethyst stone, the crystallization of the Violet energy, has the function of restoring things to their natural state. The Violet energy has the potential to soothe sores and wounds on many levels. Within the Violet is often contained great suffering and pain. It is the suffering within the joy; the bitterness within the romance. It can indicate deep grief and pain in accepting life on earth.

The gift within the Violet is the possibility of bringing Heaven to earth: in grief, there may be a desire to escape, to go back to Heaven. There may be great difficulty in coming to terms with the material aspect of existence. This may manifest as an over-indulgence in earthly pursuits, and lead to addictions, or it might appear as a tendency towards escapism and a refusal to take responsibility for the material and practical. On a spiritual or mental level the addictions may manifest as obsession, particularly religious obsession. There might be great spiritual pride and grandiosity, or a state of aloofness or detachment which leads to separation. On an emotional level this separation may show itself as profound introversion, a tendency to withdraw into neurosis and hypersensitivity where there have been deep wounds. While the combination of Red and Blue has the potential to bring great energy into the communication, the reverse may also occur. The Red is hidden within the Blue and may suggest unspoken frustration. The Violet may be an indication that there has been too much thinking which has caused great pain.

Yet within the Violet is also contained the possibility for the atonement of grief: the sense of atoning for past wrongs and mistakes and finding peace. Thus we may come to a sense of oneness with ourselves, with the Source, and with others.

Violet, too, is the colour of balance. It is the reconciliation of polarities: male and female; hot and cold; Heaven and earth; activity and thought. In a balanced state the Violet is a sign of great wholeness: the completion which occurs when we approach our own inner marriage, the inner balancing of complementary energetic forces: male and female, reason and intuition, giving and receiving. The choice of Violet may indicate a quietly balanced person who is content to give service without acknowledgement, coming as he does from a sense of his own inner completeness. It may be someone who naturally succeeds without the need to push.

There is also, within Violet, great strength. The Violet person is someone with dedication and commitment to high ideals. This is a deeply thinking person whose ideological concerns override any concern for themselves. The sacrifice within the Violet is a necessary part of the whole, since the spiritual considerations of service, healing and spirituality are more important to this person than self-gratification. This is often someone who has borne great suffering, but who, in a state of balance, is also powerful, focused and clear.

Violet is the colour of transformation, and transmutation. With the beginning of an inner sense of wholeness, and the bringing of Heaven to earth, comes the possibility of profound change. The end of a cycle implies the death of what we were in order to make way for something new. Violet is cleansing and it is purifying. St Germain is best known for his association with the lilac flame of transmutation: the deep purification of the lead of our lower and denser nature to the Gold of our true aura and potential.

The journey towards the awakening of the seventh chakra is a long one. It signifies the final reconciliation of all the opposing forces as they combine at the crown, and brings the complete relationship with all that is. This is something which has only happened in the case of such very rare beings as Christ or Buddha or Mohammed.

In all senses, Violet signifies the end of a process; and with the ending, the possibility, ultimately, of the fullest illumination and rebirth.

Roy

Bottle No. 16: Violet/Violet – the Violet Robe – contains the potential for deep change and transformation. It indicates someone who has a strong connection with the Divine plan, and is chosen by those involved in helping others in the transformative process; quite often those working with the dying. When presented as a challenge it suggests that there may be a difficulty in accepting change and in letting go of old habits.

Roy was a student attending a workshop at the time that his father was in hospital after a stroke. His father, Fred, was in his eighties and it was clear that physical recovery was extremely unlikely. When Fred was not unconscious, he was fretful and uncomfortable and clearly having great difficulty in coping with the experience. Roy took him a Violet/Violet bottle and offered it to him and, although he had no knowledge of *Aura-Soma*, Fred reached out and took it. From that time on Fred wanted to hold it, which he did for much of the time for the next three days. During this time he became much calmer. At the end of these three days he died peacefully.

INITIATION

Death and dying, and deep transformation: in one way the Violet marks the end of a process. Yet in every ending there is contained the potential for a beginning; the possibility, perhaps, of going deeper into a process to find greater understanding.

For so many of us, endings are a time of grief: the loss of a way of life which has been long familiar may involve bereavement or separation; even the leaving of a familiar home is frequently painful. Endings can be times of stark loneliness when our faith is sorely tested.

Such was the time in my journey, some months after Stephen's recovery. Grateful as I was for the warmth of the children, single parenting is nevertheless a lonely job and the scarcity of funds made it monotonous, for them and for me. I had begun to wonder whether any other destiny lay ahead.

June gave way to a beautiful and warm July. It was Saturday morning. Magdalen, six by this time, had just gone next door to play with a friend. I went to see that all was well and they were happily planning a game. Two minutes later her friend ran into our cottage screaming, 'Magdalen has been run over.'

Everything went into slow motion then. When I got to

where Magdalen was lying, all I could do was what came quietly and automatically: rest my hand gently on her back and pray for help; ask to be used as a vessel through which might come any energy she could use. Healing seemed so natural. Anything more practical was beyond me. Later I discovered that a near neighbour had already arrived and kept her air passage open: without that first aid she would certainly have died. I stayed beside her tiny body lying so serenely on the road while people gathered and the emergency services were set smoothly and brilliantly into action. I watched her as she appeared to vomit blood, and I assumed she was dying. She was not vomiting, I discovered later: she was choking on the blood from her tongue which she had severed but for a thread.

Within a few minutes Mike was beside me on the road. I overrode the well intentioned protests of the local police officer as Mike gently felt Magdalen from the base of her spine to her head. 'If she dies it's OK,' I said to Mike as we waited for the ambulance.

I thought in my initial numbness that I had investigated the depths and accepted the very worst that fate could dish out, the one thing which I had always prayed would never happen. Yet I knew that no force of Heaven or Hell could separate me from this child. Mike said then that he felt sure she was going to survive. It is the only time, bar one other, that he has told me anything he has seen of the future. I knew he saw it often and communicated it almost never. This gave me the faith that moves mountains. From that moment I scarcely ever knew doubt. Choruses of angels and men would unite, bringing Heaven to earth in the determination that this child's life could be saved.

The first of these angels, after the neighbour who had kept open Magdalen's air passage, were the emergency service staff who arrived by ambulance. They headed off at a steady 70 miles per hour to the major hospital 50 miles away; even the mile-long bridge over the Humber estuary was at the ready: it was kept open and clear of traffic to make way for their coming. Every minute counted: they used the time in the ambulance not only in keeping Magdalen alive but in shaving her head ready for the brain surgeon the other end.

By the time we came to see her in hospital the first brain operation was complete: she was wrapped up like a tiny Egyptian mummy attached to the latest life-saving technology. Magdalen's father was there. The surgeon spoke to us both, letting us know of his doubt in the possibility of saving her life, and telling us that if they were able to do so that permanent brain damage had certainly already been incurred and that it would remain only to assess the extent of it.

If ever a person was intended to survive, Magdalen must have been. If there is a Divine plan, every force in Heaven was set in motion to orchestrate the perfect symphony: a great, organic generator had been switched on where every instrument, every part, was in perfect working order and in perfect harmony with the other. This hospital, the nearest major one to where we lived, was currently the best in the country for brain surgery; the latest machinery had arrived only a month before, being the most sophisticated available. The intensive care nurses were two of the most loving, dedicated, human beings I have ever been privileged to meet. Aaron, Mike's son, had walked this road before Magdalen; it was as if he handed her the staff. Mike and Claudia had for five years since his accident searched the country for new knowledge and skills which might in any way help Aaron, and they gave the benefit of this to Magdalen within the first week. Healers gathered from all over the world and worked either directly at her side, or from far away.

Mike was teaching the next day: a course for 40 new students. How he managed it is hard to say, since he made no attempt to sleep for at least the first three nights, keeping vigil night and day. Claudia was with me, steady and calm as a lake. The news rapidly spread beyond those new students to *Aura-Soma* throughout the world. They combined with other friends from the past and the present in a group effort of prayer and healing which was visible to Mike and tangible to me.

I still come across them from time to time: people I have never met who recognize us simply from their memory of the event. I can do nothing except to thank them from the bottom of my heart and soul.

It was a nightmare gruelling beyond description: a roller-coaster of illumination and confusion, grief and elation, hope and despair. Life and death here walked hand in hand, the one bubbling with colour and warmth, the other cold and dark as black ice. The first operation was only the beginning. But for the machines, and the loving skill of those operating them, Magdalen died a second time that night. That moment was worse by far than the original event. But she was not alone: far and wide those closely involved woke from their sleep and prayed for her. When she came through that I believe she had made her choice: she had decided to stay. If she was to survive, the surgeons must once more operate. The risk was high: the huge trauma on such a small body was potentially devastating; but the alternative was still probable death and certain disability. There was no real choice.

Five days later Magdalen emerged for a few minutes from her coma. Smiling in joyful recognition, she offered just enough reassurance to help the rest of us keep going, before returning to apparent oblivion for a further five days. There was a lot of work to be done, which would take two or three years to complete. It would still be some time before she learned to eat and drink; then she would have to rediscover our names, to learn again to talk and to walk.

We can never entirely separate cause and effect, particularly in the mysterious and infinitely complex matters of life and death, illness and health. All we can do is to look at the evidence, and at our experience; and we can listen with close attention to our intuition – the inner teacher.

How was it that Magdalen made such a rapid recovery in the face of what looked like hopeless defeat? The skill and the dedication offered by the intensive care team was extraordinary; but their astonishment at her recovery was part of the experience for all those involved. While there is not a shadow of doubt that without the massive aid of highly skilled surgery and technological expertise she would not have survived beyond a few hours at most, I feel equally certain that without the help she received on an energetic, subtle level, she would not be in the condition she is today: a lively, active, healthy 10-year-old, reading and writing, running about and chattering like any other child.

On the day of the accident a friend, whose auric sight and clairvoyant faculties are highly developed, described Magdalen's aura. He said it was literally shattered, resembling a stained glass window which had been smashed and then stirred in a glass of water. It was about as far away as it is possible to be from the ideal of the rainbow being in perfect balance and harmony (*see* Plate 21).

For the duration of her coma Magdalen was fairly thoroughly incarcerated in bandages and equipment which made her body largely inaccessible. We worked gently wherever we could reach her, particularly on her feet, feeding through them any energy her body could use to mend itself. We worked on the aura too, in the same way as I had previously done with Stephen, in the hope of restoring a little of the balance which had been shattered by the shock.

Yet this event was a new dimension of experience. I was treading ground I would not have expected to explore in my worst nightmare. I had little to work with except prayer, my instinct, and my hands. I had also, by this time, learned something about the power of thought. This resulted in a passionate concern to keep the energy around her gentle and steady and unexceptionally positive. I informed only those people whom I felt I could count on to work with total faith and trust. In other words I attempted to create an atmosphere which was free of all fear. In practice this was only partially possible, and at the times when the machines registered mounting brain pressure and several extra doctors and nurses gathered round I could only usefully absent myself, hoping that distance would provide her with at least a little protection against my inevitable dread. It was made more feasible by the support of all the friends who visited, bringing with them their various healing skills; and by those further afield who were so actively helping. The healing energy they sent was as tangible as anything I have ever experienced: Pink, warm, infinitely and unconditionally loving.

The idea of a quality of energy which we can touch and feel is really pretty familiar to us all. Here, within that hospital ward, is only a more extreme example of something which many people are more or less aware of in their own experience. We know how an atmosphere around a hostile person can feel as cold as ice; or how tension in a room can feel so tight that one could almost cut through it with a knife. This was the opposite extreme. The room in which Magdalen lay took on an atmosphere of the Inner Temple in a very sacred place. This intensive care unit, with all its hi-tech metal, was indeed a holy place. This was a time when everyone united towards a passionately shared goal. The intensive-care nurses, themselves so skilled and loving, watched and listened fascinated as we worked. We all combined our knowledge and skills in harmony and with a deep mutual respect.

I knew, too, that on some level Magdalen was working as hard as the rest of us to reunite her body with her spirit. Often

I talked to her. At other times I left her to rest. When I talked to her I told her how much we all loved her; I planned with her a newly painted Pink bedroom; I talked about the party we would have for her when she was better; I read her extracts from her favourite stories. Through most of the first night a friend watched the machines which monitored the levels of pressure on the brain. Each time I talked about something she liked the pressure levels made a significant drop. Her very favourite topic of conversation appeared to be the party. Then on the fifth day when I held her in my lap all day and she offered that smiling flick of recognition, she murmured, only just audibly, the words 'mummy', 'party' and 'ice-cream' before slipping once more into the deepest sleep.

Then, little by little, the bandages were removed. Our friend's description of Magdalen's shattered aura inspired us to massage the *Balance* bottle of the appropriate colour to each area of the body, restoring the balance of colour from the very beginning of Magdalen's period of recovery. For some time we did this at frequent intervals throughout the day. Could it be that the assistance given to the aura in re-establishing its balance was part of what accounted for the astonishing speed of her recovery?

We have examined the suggestion that it is through the aura that the physical body is constantly being created and recreated. Vicky Wall taught that any attempt at true healing must take account of the aura and chakras. Any attempt at healing which ignores these dimensions is likely to be only a temporary fix. The imbalance will soon return, either as the same symptom repeated over and over again, or as a deeper one. The example of Magdalen in this connection could on the face of it seem a little irrelevant. Here we are looking at a traffic accident. It was her body, not just her aura, which was hit by a car. Nevertheless, her treatment, from the very beginning, included the rebalancing of the aura.

The second occasion on which the state of Magdalen's aura was described and drawn was three weeks after the initial impact. The auragraph shows some very considerable re-formation (*see* Plate 22).

In fact the changes are astounding. The aura has begun to re-form: chakras are forming above her head, suggesting perhaps the strong link with the spiritual realms who have undoubtedly been guiding her towards recovery. Others are forming below her feet. Does this perhaps show the connection with earth as she re-enters her body? Here is another interesting confirmation of the process in which she had been involved: a few days after our return home I was showing some photographs to a friend. They were of the various scenes in the hospital, and they naturally included several of Magdalen, unrecognizable in her battered state, her head shorn and bandaged, wires everywhere. The photographs also included a few taken several weeks before the accident when she had been riding a beach donkey. Magdalen had never seen any of these photographs, nor had she been exposed to a mirror up to this point in her convalescence. She came to look, as I showed them to my friend, and exclaimed at each of the bandaged ones: 'That's me; that's me; that's me.'

Then we came to one taken on the beach, her long hair flowing behind her. The expression on her face changed. Any trace of recognition vanished. 'Who's that?' she asked.

She had now, however, embarked on the journey back into physical life, as healing progressed and the vehicle of her body strengthened. Thus it was that as the days turned to weeks she came into an awareness of her new state. Seeing herself one day in a mirror, looking like a tattered and only half-shaven Buddha, she flew into a rage of bewilderment and grief, asking me why I had cut off her hair.

There was much work still to be done. The picture of her aura, while demonstrating enormous changes, also reflected the extent of the damage still needing to be repaired. Hence the unevenness in the colours between the different sides of the body; and the jagged edges.

Another auric picture of her was drawn two months later (*see* Plate 23). This picture shows that the rainbow-like formation which had begun to show above Magdalen's head two months previously had by this time extended its reach down her body. Everything indicates her return to earth. The jagged edges are disappearing and the colours are becoming more evenly balanced.

The event of a split second of time can bring to an end the whole of life as we knew it to be. As we had stood on the road waiting for the ambulance Mike had said to me, 'There *is* a Divine plan. The trouble is that we don't know what it is.'

Nor, often, do we understand very much of its purpose. I know only that there are occasions when it seems necessary for one person to sacrifice themselves in order that others may learn. There is no doubt that this incident brought a new level of communication between many people, and a quantum leap towards faith and trust.

I do not yet know what it has brought Magdalen: only time will tell. Head injuries, apparently, often act as a stimulus to the higher faculties, opening people up to clairvoyance, clairaudience and so on; not that anyone would wish such an experience on anyone for all the deep seeing in the world. But as the years have gone by, some of the lessons, and even the gifts, within the experience have come gradually to light, prompting me towards a deepening of my understanding, and raising my awareness towards those other dimensions, reminding me that we are never really alone. This was, in some sense, initiation.

It was, in no uncertain terms, the end of one process. It was also the beginning of something new. For all the pain, there is the certain knowledge that from the moment of impact life would never be the same again. Energy moves in spirals, like the smoke from a candle. So, I believe, it is with us as we gradually learn and evolve. We repeat something of the same processes, but we view them from a different place. So, for a while, the issue of survival, in every sense, would be a challenge more pressing than it had ever been. Yet the doubt had vanished. And Christ was with us all the way – visible, audible, and tangible – carrying Magdalen in one arm while holding my hand with the other. I believe from my own experience and from all that she told me, as her faculty of speech returned, of her conversations with God, that such an event opens up the way for many more towards a personal experience of Christ.

And so to the last stage of one journey, where we move above and beyond the realms of the physical body, to the Magenta above the crown of the head; and finally to the Clear, or the pure White light.

MAGENTA

Beyond the physical body, above the crown chakra, there exists another new colour: the Magenta. Like the Turquoise, the other 'New Age' ray, the Magenta offers us the promise of things to come. Unseen before Goethe glimpsed at its hidden power, it may now, from time to time, be faintly perceived beneath the Violet at the bottom of the rainbow.

Magenta is a complex energy, deep-rooted, powerful and strong. Its presence above the crown denotes another newly-awakening chakra: the eighth one. This is the beginning of a new cycle, where the Blue once again merges into and becomes contained within the Red. Here we have one part Blue to two parts Red; and yet the Red energy, which hitherto has been so overtly earthly and physical, now creates the space above and beyond the physical within which the soul star, the Divine Blueprint of our incarnation, may expand and find manifestation. Perhaps this is part of the explanation for the complex character of this energy.

This new ray is unfamiliar to us in the contemporary world. We have few symbols with which to explain its nature. It features more in the art of Native American Indians and other small-scale cultures. Magenta dye was the first of the synthetic dyes to be made from coal tar, and its striking impact made it very popular among fashionable Parisian women at the turn of the twentieth century.

Magenta is, indeed, a very arresting colour. It is, for one thing, a curious combination of the energies of Red and of Pink, containing all the passion and commitment of the Red with all the tenderness of the Pink. Part of its essence could be described as 'passionate tenderness', or 'unconditional passion'. In addition to this it contains, as we have seen, something of the Blue: Magenta is the energizing and grounding of the Blueprint.

Beyond all this, Magenta actually contains, hidden within its depths, all the other colours of the spectrum. It exists within the *Aura-Soma* range in two forms: one is a hue, similar in intensity to most of the other colours displayed in the *Balance* bottles; the other would be better described as a shade, a very much deeper and darker colour, so dark that it appears black until a light is shone through it to reveal its rich and unusual beauty. Where the pure White light reflects all the colours of the spectrum, Magenta has all those colours contained. Thus it represents the limitless darkness out of which comes all light, all creation. The Magenta in this deep dark form comprises the base fraction in a number of *Balance* bottles known as Rescue combinations. It is a profoundly healing energy brought, within these combinations, into various contexts where it may respond to one or another crisis. Within the deep richness which this dark Magenta hides is contained the full spectrum of healing rays. When we are drawn to these combinations we display not only our need for profound healing but also at some unconscious level our recognition of the fullness of the potential which lies dormant within the depths of ourselves. It is a reminder that the answers, when once we can access them, lie within.

Such is the power and strength of the Magenta ray that the

Magenta paint developed by Dr Castellani is disinfectant, anti-septic and anti-fungal purely on the potency of its colour. Vicky Wall used this paint successfully in her physical healing work to treat Athlete's Foot.

The love in Magenta may express itself in numerous ways. It may create a harmonious state of human felicity; it may be expressed as a state of love and creativity tinged with sadness, the kind of sweet melancholy vocalized in the music, for example, of Edith Piaf. The choice of Magenta sometimes indicates underlying difficulties within the nuclear family: there may have been either 'smother love' in the past (and maybe in the present), or the complete absence of love on any level which has prompted the person at an early stage of their life to turn to spiritual sources of nourishment. The Magenta conceals a lot of Red: with the passion there may also be anger around the issue of love.

Magenta is the colour of love on many levels; particularly the Divine. It can show an intense love for humanity; a vehement love for God. It brings to our attention the need to invest the quality of love and care in the details. When we can put love into the little things we reflect something of the energy behind the Divine creation, which pays attention to the smallest particulars. Magenta is an energy through which we may bring quality into the way we live.

This energy has, therefore, also to do with the possibility of awakening to beauty. Yet even within this there may be pain. Within the Magenta is great love and also, sometimes, great suffering. It is an energy whose light and essence must be used sparingly and cautiously. To be deeply sensitive to beauty may also involve a painful awareness of suffering. Magenta is a karmic colour that reaches into the very depths of man's and woman's memory and may bring forward karmic issues which are unsolved, bringing them to the surface of our memory and thought and feeling. The essence of Magenta is elemental and, like the flame, it can cast light but it can also burn.

So, within the darkness of Magenta, is great nurturing and learning, but also anguish and isolation. Magenta, above even the Violet, can indicate in one choosing it a very great desire to 'go home', to escape from life on earth.

Yet, at its highest, Magenta is the Divine love, the food from the gods which nourishes us at the deepest level. It is Divine healing which restores our faith and our well-being; and which can connect us with our deepest truth and the purpose which brought us into this life. Hence it may bring us towards our right livelihood, aligning us with the appropriate activity in which we may invest our energy to bring us fulfilment and prosperity. Although Magenta can mean the need for sacrifice, the letting go of life energy, the surrendering of blood, it can also indicate sacrificial love in the most positive sense: the Red of love merged with the Blue of service can lead us towards the fulfilment of love freely offered in the service of others. Some clairvoyants have said that this ray was strongly seen around Christ on his crucifixion.

So while there is a lot of sacrifice in the Magenta, and the choice of it may indicate the deep need for love, it is also the ability to offer love at the highest level.

Magenta is also about being appropriate in each moment: when we invest enough love in the small things – the care for an ailing butterfly or the tending of the plants or the avoidance of harsh products which damage the ecological balance – then the love will always be available, as in a deposit account, in ample supply. This love may then be applied with great precision in a way which is appropriate to each situation. Magenta also has, therefore, the property of stimulating our attention; particularly in relation to spirituality.

Magenta, representing the beginning of a new cycle, is a colour associated with inspirational thinkers: those living ahead of their time whose talents and perceptions ease humanity towards a new and higher vibration. Goethe, having been the first to recognize the Magenta ray, provides an example of this: so do many of the great musicians and artists whose vision raised the awareness of mankind to new levels of perception.

Magenta, once the difficulties of physical life are accepted, may be peaceful, stable, soothing; it may be the profound nurturing of feminine love at its most intuitive and creative. It is, in some ways, the death of the old order and the progression towards the new wave of a new age.

Children, being clearer and less cluttered than we are, have a straightforwardness and a purity of vision which has much to teach us. On a workshop a while ago Magdalen, and Lilleth, Claudia and Mike's daughter, came after school to join in for a short time. The group I was with were working on Magenta. One of the students asked the children what they thought of when they looked at the Magenta/Magenta bottle. They replied, instantly and together.

'I think of angels,' said Lilleth.

'I think of Jesus,' said Magdalen.

Out of the mouths of babes... perception and understanding, and the beginning of a new cycle.

CLEAR

Where the Magenta contains the full spectrum of colours in potential, the Clear radiates and shines out this spectrum of light.

The Clear, or the pure White light, exists above and beyond and around the rainbow. It is the blank page in which all colour is kept. It is the father and mother of light, from which all colour is conceived. The Clear is combined light: through Clear light the rainbow is born prismically, each colour stacked upon the other in perfect balance and harmony.

We can gain much insight into the nature of the Clear light from its name. The name implies clarity: the phrase 'crystal clear' portrays the purity of Clear quartz crystal, which is the solidification of pure light. It illustrates crystal glass equally well. Both these substances are transparent: they allow all the light to come through them, offering the possibility of clear sight. The Clear light, when shone on a problem, affords us the opportunity for clarity and deep understanding. Clear offers clarification and illumination to whatever is placed under its beam.

Conversely, the Clear has the potential to reflect, like a mirror, all that is placed in front of it, giving the receiver the

opportunity of recognizing himself. Thus, immediately, we see within the Clear a paradox. Will the light enter and penetrate, bringing forth all that has been hidden in the darkness? In such cases the selection of a proportion of the colour which we refer to as Clear may suggest that the person has chosen a path of clarification in life: a path which brings cleansing and comprehension, and which has probably involved deep suffering. Or will the light all be reflected back to its source, so that nothing is revealed? In this case the choice of Clear may indicate the need to remain invisible.

The power of the Clear light is symbolized by the full moon. The moon has no light of its own, but reflects the light of the sun. It shines at night; and when it is full it sheds the greatest light on the subconscious, illuminating those thoughts and emotions which at other times remain concealed.

Clear is about intensity. The Clear energy amplifies all that it touches, just as Clear quartz crystal has the property of magnifying energy. Its selection indicates an intensity of suffering and experience above all the other colours. When a Clear fraction appears in conjunction with a chakra colour, it shows pressing issues around that energy centre.

The choice of Clear, particularly near the beginning of a selection, may suggest that 'the tears have washed all the colour from my life'. The person may be simply wrung out, and perhaps physically drained, by grief. Or it may imply that there is a well of unshed tears; a need to let go of deep suffering. It might occasionally indicate the deepest of rage, as in the clenching of fists to the point where the knuckles turn White. Or it may mean that the person has undergone a deep cleansing process and is now ready to come into their true colours.

This may be a good place to be, even when it is uncomfortable. The purification may have brought us to the point where we understand why it is that we suffer. This is the

point where it becomes possible to access the wisdom within the suffering. Vicky Wall referred frequently to 'the pearl within the oyster-bed of suffering'. This understanding can lead to the possibility of karmic absolution: when the lesson is fully learned there is no further need to endure the pain. Thus we can participate consciously in the purification process. Then as this process of cleansing unfolds and develops, we can begin to build a body of light and transcend the limitations of the physical body. The White rose is the symbol of purified love. It is a reminder that it is love which opens the door to the process of refinement.

There are times when we prefer to ignore the shadow; to deny those aspects of ourselves which we do not wish to examine. This is when the Clear becomes a process of reflecting back outwards all that we would wish not to see. This is the denial of a part of ourselves. It is exemplified in over-processed foods such as White bread or White sugar, which are attractively presented at the expense, perhaps, of wholeness and wholesomeness.

The White snow and the Clear ice are both forms of frozen water; and water is the element which is associated with emotion. Thus the Clear may symbolize frozen emotion. A thaw will be necessary before the emotion may be expressed. Snow is also a symbol of purity: 'pure as the driven snow'.

Snow may also, like White sugar and bread, symbolize the denial of whatever lies beneath when it displays itself as an attractive package. A well-known caution to those buying a house is to avoid choosing it either in fresh snow, or bright sunshine (another manifestation of the Clear White light), when we might well be tempted to ignore its shadow side!

Like the Magenta, Clear implies a wide potential. All the colours are reflected herein, and someone drawn to the Clear energy may have a clear and a broad mind. This may be someone with a powerful intellect which could equally be

applied to questions of philosophy, mathematics or the arts. It may be someone with a high idealism; perhaps a touch of puritanism. As a strength the Clear might demonstrate a state of poised and confident equilibrium, just as the rainbow exists in harmony and balance. Within such equilibrium is the possibility of a full rich world: prisms and butterflies' wings and all the diamond lights, shining and flickering, ever-changing in the brightness of sunshine. Within the Clear is the potential for a kaleidoscope of creativity and experience.

Clear, perhaps more than the other colours, contains a paradox. It may indicate, as a difficulty, a sense of emptiness; or, as a gift, a feeling of spaciousness. It may be transparency or reflection. It may be the deepest well of grief and tears or profound equanimity. It contains the duality which comes from the source of all light. Clear is the head and the godhead of colour. It is the sun and the moon, and the shining brightness of stars.

Maybe, in the context of the journey, the Clear may be seen as the light at the end of the tunnel, the resolution of the difficulties on the way, as all the myriad colours, with their challenges and their gifts, reunite. The light at the end of the tunnel is the star that leads us on, offering us hope eternal, and understanding; inspiring and uplifting us, that we may find the courage to open our eyes and expand our hearts.

TREADING THE DAWN

Here, then, is the end of one of many many journeys. For me, many new journeys were beginning, when I would take the colours to far-flung corners of the world – places which would have seemed to me even more unlikely than Lincolnshire had been at the beginning of this process. All over the world people are waking up to the illuminating, healing power of colour. They soak up the energies of light and burst into flower like the almond tree of St Francis.

The journey through the hues and the tints of the rainbow, and the understanding of some of the experiences that each one contains, is only the beginning of *Aura-Soma*. The aim of this book has been to paint a portrait of *Aura-Soma*, and to illustrate the language of colour which is its fundamental tool.

Since its birth some 14 years ago, *Aura-Soma* has grown in depth and breadth, throwing light on all that it touches. The founder, Vicky Wall, living with her colleague on their meagre joint pensions, never borrowed a penny nor advertised; yet by the time of her death seven years later this system was being practised on all five continents. It seems that it travels of its

own accord to wherever it is needed. Since those early days much more of the wisdom hidden within it has been understood. Constantly more is being revealed. There is the possibility, in the future, of many more journeys, where we may go ever deeper, further and further towards the source.

Already *Aura-Soma* has been found to overlap and correspond with many other systems of wisdom, some of them very ancient. The main primary colours according to Goethe, for example, relate to the major constitutional types recognized in homoeopathy. The Yogic view of the trinity of energies also corresponds to the primary colours, and has much to teach us of the evolution of consciousness. Buddhist philosophy recognizes three main tendencies within human behaviour, which relate precisely to colour. So do the ancient sciences of Numerology and Astrology. Most significantly of all, perhaps, is the profound and astonishing link with the Kabbalistic Tree of Life, a 'mind map' of human consciousness, and possibly the most ancient system of wisdom available to man.

All these are introduced to students moving through a training programme. Nevertheless, the fundamental tool is a deep understanding of the language of colour, through which the intuition may then begin to flow.

In the years since the birth of *Aura-Soma* there have been countless numbers of situations in which the application of colour has been followed by results on the physical and energetic level which are little short of miraculous. Such cases were witnessed from the beginning by Vicky Wall, and described in her book *The Miracle of Colour Healing*. They have also been experienced since by the many thousands of people around the world practising, teaching, or simply using this system of colour. More than 14 years of evidence exists to show that *Aura-Soma* frequently produces profound healing effects on the physical level, but I would like to emphasize an important point we have reached in our understanding of

Aura-Soma as it has grown and developed. This is that it seems on closer inspection that the greater purpose of *Aura-Soma* is contained not so much within its effects as a healing system but more in its capacity to bring about a gentle modification in consciousness. This, ultimately, will promote deeper and more permanent changes in our way of life and our understanding; and will doubtless also repercuss upon the physical level. The physical effects, the consequence of rebalancing and awakening on the higher levels of our consciousness, warrant less attention than the consciousness aspect, as we attempt to understand *Aura-Soma*.

Over and over again we are reminded in *Aura-Soma* that we are the colours we choose, and that the colours we choose reflect our being's needs. In ordinary circumstances, *Aura-Soma* is a system whereby the individual chooses the colours to which he or she is most drawn. It is only in some of the unusual circumstances described in the text – accidents, for example, or times when for one reason or another the person needing help is unable to choose their colours for themselves – that we will choose for them. A vital characteristic of *Aura-Soma*, let us remember, is the single feature which sets this system apart from other therapies: the fact that it is self-selective. In choosing our colours we are discovering for ourselves the deeper aspects of whatever imbalances we display. We are also *choosing our own remedy*. This is really very important. *Aura-Soma* is currently the only system available which hands back entirely to the client the responsibility for their own healing process, and which thus seems to be so singularly in tune with the movement into a new state of consciousness.

In offering any consultation the therapist may, through the client's choice of bottles, assist in creating an atmosphere in which that person may feel free to be entirely themselves. This is a great gift we may offer one another. The counsellor

provides guidance and insight about the possible reasons why we are drawn to the colours we have selected, but does not choose them for us. This is a very different situation from the one we are accustomed to in so many circumstances, in which we hand over our responsibility to an outside expert. Thus *Aura-Soma* offers us something most unexpected: an encounter with *Balance* becomes an opportunity for us to discover that no other individual knows more about us than our unconscious mind already knows for itself! *Aura-Soma* offers us the opportunity to begin to access some of that information and bring it, literally, into the light.

It seems that when we are faced with the possibility of choosing a few bottles from 98 different colour combinations, what is happening is that the unconscious or soul aspect of ourselves is entering into a relationship, a kind of conversation, with the colours in front of us. During much of our busy lives we are alienated from the higher aspects of our consciousness and it is easy to slip out of touch with our needs. We stay, perhaps, in touch with our desires; but this is something which is often very different from our needs. We accumulate layers of conditioning which separate us from our own essential truth. It is this essential truth which is reflected in our choice of colours and, if we could but see them, in the colours we radiate.

It may well be that the experience of recognizing our colours this way has something in common with what we experience at the moment of death. The evidence of those who have come close to this themselves is that we experience a direct encounter with the totality of ourselves. It appears also that at this moment, without the use of our eyes, the consciousness perceives colour directly. All of the various religious traditions as well as modern researchers have documented the essential feature of a near death experience as an experience of colour; even the sequence in which the

colours are experienced appears to be the same in every case. This re-affirms the fundamental point that we are beings of colour and light; that even without the sensory organs of perception, our eyes, we experience colour directly. Individuals who have recently been near to death are more closely in contact with the soul aspect of themselves, and thus they tend to be more accurately attuned to their being's needs.

Thus Magdalen, while bravely attempting to return to the full-time occupation of her body, was acutely aware of her needs in relation to colour. Unable to speak, or to stand for more than a short time, she crawled around the floor displaying considerable anxiety until she was able to find the only clothes she would agree to wear: a Violet T-shirt and Pink leggings, which interestingly were of the same hue almost precisely as the colours of the *Balance* bottle which had been placed behind her head throughout the whole time in which she had been unconscious. For several weeks this outfit had to be washed every night; without it she could find no peace, despite the several other new clothes she had been offered.

On many levels this time marked, for us, as I have said, the end of one process and the movement towards something new. The last of our remaining 'capital' consisted of a few jewels: the final link, for a while, with the trappings of materialism. These jewels went to London to be sold. This was primarily because Magdalen's choice of foods was as clear in its colour coding as had been her choice of clothes. Her need for high-quality foods was clear; but it was only she who knew, each day, the necessary colours. For many joyful weeks Magdalen ate the quantity and quality of foods she required: strawberries, raspberries, red meat, orange peppers, green peas. By pointing to the foods she needed, for some months she effectively did her own shopping.

Nearly three years later she was with me at an *Aura-Soma* event in Tokyo. Living by this time a life pretty much like

other children, she was very rarely involved in my work. The angels which she had drawn or painted for the first six months or so of her recovery, to the exclusion of all else, had now given way to trees and flowers. Most of the time she simply played with her toys, her only contact with *Balance* being to make potions from it and smother it over her dolls. To help her to stave off any boredom while I worked at this event in Tokyo, a kind friend offered her a gift of three very small naked celluloid dolls. I noticed with some surprise that she played perfectly peacefully all day long, despite the noise and the large crowds, arranging and re-arranging these little plastic people around a display of *Balance* bottles. She commented casually at the end of the day that she had called these new dolls her angel babies because they had been playing in Heaven all day.

'You see', she explained to me, 'that is how I imagine Heaven to be.'

Was this mere child's play? Possibly; but I would not be so certain.

So life is an adventure: the advent of spirit into the dense realms of what we experience as the material world, where light energy has in many places become so concentrated that it seems for all the world to be solidity itself. Indeed, within this solid dimension the light is often not apparent. The torch is extinguished and we voyage, sometimes, in the dark. We sail through gorges and narrow straits, we make our homes in thick undergrowth and dimly-lit caves; we scale mountains and skim the deepest oceans in our explorations. The light glimmers and twinkles, darting and dancing in constant interplay with all upon which it beams.

Part of the journey is to explore the darkness: to discover the other side of the light. We walk in the shadow and learn what it has to teach us. When the light grows dim it becomes hard for us to see our way, and so we make mistakes. We lose

our sense of direction and maybe we even lose the map. The journey becomes a test: can we find our way to the next post? Will we remember this mistake and avoid that pitfall in the future? Well maybe sometimes we will and sometimes we won't. Then the drawing of another day, bringing new light. We can survey the landscape and see where we took a wrong turn. 'Pain', suggested C.S. Lewis, 'is God's megaphone to rouse a deaf world.'

So we may tread the dawn of each new experience a little stronger, with more knowledge. The understanding grows deeper, as the light penetrates, little by little, the dense darkness which is a part of ourselves. But maybe this is only the outward journey. This voyage, outward-bound, is in the largest possible sense the voyage of growing up.

Does it not seem, therefore, that as we make the return journey to the Source of light from which we came, we bring the light of experience and understanding to each energy centre in succession so that in apprehending the reality of ourselves we begin to find true communication with one another? As each of the chakras responds to 'God's megaphone', we may learn to hear and to see things as they really are. It is only in recognizing and listening to ourselves that we may learn to offer the same quality of recognition to our fellow hue-man beings.

As we journey on, treading the dawn of a new era, we experience, moment to moment, the gift of each new breath; each new day. Sometimes we are joyful; sometimes quietly content. At other times we are full of questions, and sometimes full of doubts. Perhaps, if we are willing to look, colour will throw its light on those questions, and help us to find the answers. Then we can let go of the confusion and the doubt and walk tall, all chakras exposed to the light, moving onward and upward in faith and trust.

USEFUL ADDRESSES

The author teaches *Aura-Soma* at Foundation, Intermediate and Advanced levels in the UK and other countries.

From her home in Oxford she works, through the medium of colour, with individuals and groups in a variety of counselling situations. She also runs workshops specifically for couples who want to deepen or re-balance their relationships.

For further information you may contact Philippa at her e-mail address:

merivale@globalnet.co.uk

There are three *Aura-Soma* centres established around the world. The first of these is in Tetford, Lincolnshire. The two which have grown up since are in Texas and New South Wales. Information about the training programme both in England and internationally may be obtained from:

Aura-Soma
South Road
Tetford
Horncastle
Lincolnshire
LN9 6QB
England
Tel: 44 (0) 1507 533581
Fax: 44 (0) 1507 533412

Information may also be obtained regarding counsellors within the UK.

Lucia Angelis is *Aura-Soma*'s retail outlet in London. All staff are qualified counsellors and can therefore offer consultations and advice regarding the appropriate products. *Balance,*

Pomanders and *Quintessences* are available; in addition to these there are many supporting products.

SOME INTERNATIONAL *AURA-SOMA* CONTACTS

Austria
Hanni Reichlin-Meldegg
Tel: 43 1368 8787
Fax: 43 1368 1968

Australia
Marg & Harry Simon
Tel: 61 29541 1066
Fax: 61 29543 0240

Belgium
Elizabeth de Jonge
Tel/Fax: 32 2772 8597

Brazil
Regina Kinzer (Puja)
Tel: 55 71332 2048
Fax: 55 71245 7149

Margarita Schack
Tel: 55 32355 1140
Fax: 55 32355 1139

Canada
Lynn Robinson
Tel/Fax: 1 604469 4886

Denmark
Elly Hinz
Tel: 45 3325 2930
Fax: 45 3122 3577

France
Sandra Bartin
Tel/Fax: 32 1391 69181

Italy
Robert Hasinger
Tel: 39 6884 1534
Fax: 39 68530 1829

Japan
Gatasansa
Tel: 81 4672 35683
Fax: 81 4672 31968

Netherlands
Mensys
Tel: 31 23529 1174
Fax: 31 23547 1196

Norway
Raji and Madhuri
Tel: 47 2214 2025
Fax: 47 2214 2114

New Zealand
Brenda Stanford
Tel: 64 9478 1311
Fax: 64 9478 1312

South Africa
Melissie Jolly
Tel/Fax: 27 31764 5455

Spain
Sheila Bearne de Martin
Tel/Fax: 34 1734 7237

Sweden
Christine Dilts
Tel/Fax: 46 46126 663

Monica Haeckberg
Tel/Fax: 46 8715 7622

Switzerland
Kathi Beesley
Tel: 44 31 901 0888
Fax: 41 31 901 1929

Christa Pagnotti
Tel: 41 1 241 5700
Fax: 41 1 241 5705

USA
Wil & Trish Hunter
Tel: 1 830 935 2355
Fax: 1 830 935 2508

INDEX